AF241685

MINDSET MASTERY

UNFUNK *YOUR THINKING,* **REWIRE** *YOUR BRAIN,*
AND **UNLOCK** *YOUR FULL POTENTIAL*

HANNA OLIVAS
ALONG WITH 11 INSPIRING AUTHORS

© **2025 ALL RIGHTS RESERVED**.

Published by She Rises Studios Publishing **www.SheRisesStudios.com.**

No part of this book may be reproduced or transmitted in any form whatsoever, electronic, or mechanical, including photocopying, recording, or by any informational storage or retrieval system without the expressed written, dated and signed permission from the publisher and co-authors.

LIMITS OF LIABILITY/DISCLAIMER OF WARRANTY:

The co-authors and publisher of this book have used their best efforts in preparing this material. While every attempt has been made to verify the information provided in this book, neither the co-authors nor the publisher assumes any responsibility for any errors, omissions, or inaccuracies.

The co-authors and publisher make no representation or warranties with respect to the accuracy, applicability, or completeness of the contents of this book. They disclaim any warranties (expressed or implied), merchantability, or for any purpose. The co-authors and publisher shall in no event be held liable for any loss or other damages, including but not limited to special, incidental, consequential, or other damages.

ISBN: 978-1-968061-95-1

DEDICATION

To every person who has ever felt trapped by their own mind — this book is for you. For those who have stared at the ceiling late at night, wrestling with doubt, fear, or regret, wondering if there is more to life than the cycle you are living now, we see you.

This work is dedicated to the dreamers who have been told they are unrealistic, the achievers who have felt the sting of burnout, and the quiet warriors who have fought battles no one else could see. You are proof that resilience is built in the moments when you choose to rise again, even when it would be easier to quit.

It is also for the next generation — for our children and the ones who will follow — so they may inherit not only our lessons but also our belief in the power of the human mind to adapt, grow, and thrive.

And finally, this is for those who dared to challenge their own limitations, who understood that mastery is not a destination but a daily practice. May these words serve as both a guide and a companion on your journey to becoming the highest, truest version of yourself.

Written by Hanna Olivas, Founder and CEO of She Rises Studios, Creator of SHECONOMY™, Chief Branding Officer of FENIX TV, and Adriana Luna Carlos, Co-Founder and COO of She Rises Studios and Executive Producer at FENIX TV.

TABLE OF CONTENTS

INTRODUCTION

In every season of life, we are shaped by our thoughts. They can be the silent architects of our success or the invisible chains that hold us back. Mindset is not simply a buzzword; it is the lens through which we interpret every challenge, every opportunity, and every possibility. For too long, many of us have lived with mental patterns that quietly sabotage our growth. We tell ourselves stories about what is possible, often based on fear, past experiences, or the limits others have placed on us. The truth is, those stories can be rewritten.

This book was born from the belief that your mind is your most valuable asset. With the right tools, strategies, and awareness, you can unlearn the patterns that no longer serve you, replace them with empowering beliefs, and create the life you've always envisioned. *Mindset Mastery* is not about wishful thinking or vague affirmations. It is about intentional rewiring: building mental resilience, clarity, and discipline so you can approach life with focus and confidence.

Here you will find practical techniques, proven neuroscience principles, and relatable stories that will guide you to break through the mental clutter. This is your invitation to question your current thought patterns, challenge your comfort zone, and develop a mindset that doesn't just react to life but shapes it.

By the final chapter, our goal is for you to not only believe that change is possible but to live it—with every choice, every habit, and every thought. Your future is shaped by what you think today. It is time to unfunk your thinking, rewire your brain, and unlock the full potential that has always been within you.

Written by Hanna Olivas, Founder and CEO of She Rises Studios, Creator of SHECONOMY™, Chief Branding Officer of FENIX TV, and Adriana Luna Carlos, Co-Founder and COO of She Rises Studios and Executive Producer at FENIX TV.

FOREWORD

Mindset is often spoken about in passing, as if it were a simple motivational phrase or a fleeting mood. But anyone who has transformed their life knows it is the foundation for every achievement, every breakthrough, and every moment of lasting change. When your thinking is misaligned, even the best strategies and resources will fall short. When your mindset is empowered, possibilities open where others see obstacles.

The principles you are about to explore in Mindset Mastery are not theoretical. They are built on research, personal experience, and the real-life application of methods that work. This is a book for those who are ready to take responsibility for their inner world, to stop letting outdated beliefs dictate their choices, and to start leading their life with intention.

As you read, you will notice the balance between science and story, between hard facts and practical steps. This is deliberate. Change happens when information meets action. The exercises and insights here are designed to be lived, not just read.

If you commit to the process, you will notice shifts — small at first, then undeniable — in the way you think, respond, and create. That is the essence of rewiring your brain: replacing the default settings of fear, doubt, and limitation with a blueprint for focus, growth, and possibility.

This book will not do the work for you, but it will equip you with the tools to do it yourself. And when you do, you will discover that the potential you have been seeking has been within you all along.

Written by Hanna Olivas, Founder and CEO of She Rises Studios, Creator of SHECONOMY™, Chief Branding Officer of FENIX TV, and Adriana Luna Carlos, Co-Founder and COO of She Rises Studios and Executive Producer at FENIX TV.

Hanna Olivas

Founder and CEO of SHE RISES STUDIOS

https://www.linkedin.com/company/she-rises-studios/
https://www.facebook.com/sherisesstudios
https://www.instagram.com/sherisesstudios_llc/
www.SheRisesStudios.com

Author, Speaker, and Founder. Hanna was born and raised in Las Vegas, Nevada, and has paved her way to becoming one of the most influential women of 2022. Hanna is the co-founder of She Rises Studios and the founder of the Brave & Beautiful Blood Cancer Foundation. Her journey started in 2017 when she was first diagnosed with Multiple Myeloma, an incurable blood cancer. Now more than ever, her focus is to empower other women to become leaders because The Future is Female. She is currently traveling and speaking publicly to women to educate them on entrepreneurship, leadership, and owning the female power within.

Georgene Summers

A World 4 Women
TRANSFORMATIONAL SPEAKER

https://www.linkedin.com/in/georgene-summers/
https://www.aworld4women.com
https://www.georgenesummers.com

Georgene Summers is a born entrepreneur channeling a wild streak that just won't quit. Adventurer, author, transformational speaker, life-coach, inventor, and risk-taker, the wildly animated Summers seems to have done it all. Georgene spent several highly successful decades in the fashion accessories business between Los Angeles and New York City followed by two years on Wall Street, before deciding to build a nightclub in the heart of Manhattan. Beyond trendy, Bolero, hosted many hot, happening Celebrity-filled parties. Not one to say no to challenges Georgene then built a telecommunications company with 55 successful chat lines. Since 1996 she has experienced seven safaris alone, no tours, in Africa, with only her unarmed Masai guide as company. In 2002 Georgene moved alone to Africa, something that would change her life forever. She recently completed her Memoir, "Angels In Sin, Mayhem, Money, and Murder," a page turner which was released April 2025.

Unstuck! From Fear to Fearless Mindset Reset Reboot Renew

By Georgene Summers

Have you ever stopped to wonder why you don't have that "perfect" job, home, life relationship? What is it about your mindset that stands in the way of your goals and dreams? Most of us have been brought up in the mindset of fear, where healthy fears morph into unhealthy ones that paralyze you and prevent you from living your dreams. Today you are going to change that mindset and embrace becoming a fearless warrior who says yes to all challenges and reaches their highest potential for growth and greatness every day. So it is time to change the channel of that engrained mindset, and soar like an eagle through the crevices of your life.

It is no secret that we all go through life dealing with fear to some degree or another. Some fears are healthy and serve to protect you while others are downright unrealistic, serving only to prevent you from living your dreams and reaching your highest potential for growth and greatness. Sadly, far too many people live their lives confined by the latter and are never able to jump off that proverbial cliff without a net and experience the thrill of facing fear head on and winning.

If you look back and are totally candid with yourself, I am sure you will be able to recall numerous opportunities that you allowed to pass you by because of an unreasonable and perhaps irrational fear of the unknown. Yes, that place you failed to investigate, but rather determined was too frightening, risky unknown for you to go there. Fear stops us and prevents us from living our lives to the fullest and achieving our dreams, and yet we establish a mindset that allows it to permeate our being on a regular basis.

There is nothing that contributes to failure more than the emotion of fear. It can paralyze a normally healthy person and prevent them from any type of movement. But no failure could be more intense than the failure to take action; he failure to recognize your own potential and to just allow yourself to fail without trying. You guarantee failure if you don't try and trying means the necessary steps to move forward in whatever you do. If you don't have movement and stay motionless, frozen in the fear of success or failure you have inadvertently chosen one of your fears, failure, for you have doomed yourself to fail by not risking. Why wouldn't you take risks? With risk comes reward. Without risk, you continue along the pathway to nowhere; living a life that you may someday regret. Don't be reluctant to take risks, to step off the cliff without a parachute. Life is an exciting adventure and each day should be a catalyst for men and women everywhere to expand to their fullest potential and make a difference.

I believe that in our lives, we can do anything we want or be anyone we want to be. What you need to have to accomplish this is passion and the motivation that comes with focus determination and the mental mindset that gives you the green light instead of the red one.

There is no reason that you can't do anything you set your mind on, but the passion and dedication must be present I never say no to anything, but rather follow the pathway of saying yes to all challenges and opportunitiesTruth is you don't know if you can do something or not unless you jump in with both feet and give it your best efforts. But the truth is that FEAR steps in and blocks you. Remember, there are healthy fears and unhealthy ones, and the latter are the ones that need to be replaced in your mindset.

Now is the perfect time to do a reassessment of your mindset, your core beliefs, or as I like to call it an "Autopsy of the Soul" what works and what doesn't.

What are the ules that govern your behavior? We all have rules around our emotions and what it takes to make us feel loved, rejected, sad, happy, important, valuable, angry. What emotions do you value most? Is it happiness, love, serenity, pride, inspiration, awe, gratitude, amusement, significance, hope or excitement What are the rules you have around those emotions? Think about what you need to feel those emotions. Are your rules too rigid? Does someone have to call you a dozen times a day for you to feel loved and valuable? Do your co-workers have to congratulate you constantly for a job well-done for you to feel valuable? What are the consequences for those rules? What do you value most? Is it Success, Peace, Independence, Integrity, Security, Adventure, Love, Money or something else entirely. Now look at your belief system. What core beliefs do you have that dictate your behavior? Many of these are established when we are children and so we don't even realize it. What are the consequences of those beliefs? Does your belief system guide you towards problems or new solutions? Do your beliefs focus on your power of choice or your powerlessness? Do those beliefs make you focus on the past on the presentorthe future? Just look at children being raised by religious groups with strict ideologies. Those children are brought up believing in a specific and probably strict religious code that includes for example, refusal to grant equal rights to Gay & Lesbian men women. Their core belief system is that anything outside of a man and woman together is a sin. It is drilled in from childhood and becomes an unwitting part of their core beliefs, and that is their mindset, to be intolerant of people in the LGBTQ Community. Remember, if you want to have a fulfilling life, you need to choose your beliefs carefully, and be willing to change your mindset if it does not align with your life's goals and dreams.

Back in the mid-80s, I needed a side hustle to pay for two rental properties I owned in Colorado that were not rented. I applied for a howroom job making $1500 a month at the California Mart which I thought would be easy to get as I had decades of experience in that field, operating my own highly successful Fashion Accessories showroom there. It turned out I was wrong because the company that was hiring owned five Duty Free Shops in Hong Kong and represented stellar lines like Chanel and Givenchy, and thought I was far too experienced for the position given the six-figure income I had been making in the ashion business.

Of course I was, but I did not let that deter me and instead bolstered the fact that they would be lucky getting me for such a knockdown price and after numerous phone calls they hired me. Three weeks into employment a large box arrived at the showroom which I promptly opened. Inside was a series of handbags constructed of a very trendy, rubberized material.

Unfortunately, the bags while trendy in fabric were styled for "older ladies" and none of them related, style-wise, the futuristic material they were made from.

Shortly after I opened the box, the owner arrived, and excitedly asked me what I thought of the new handbag line. Without hesitation, I replied that it looked like it was designed by a blind person and that I could create a much better line. He called me into his office and asked me what I needed to accomplish the task. Now, unbeknownst to him, I didn't know the difference between a gusset and a grommet, but I stayed on course and went home to create the perfect handbag line.

Several weeks later I returned with a large black portfolio and ten sketches of what I thought to be beautiful bags of snakeskin and lamb leather. He loved the line, but it took some convincing to get him to agree to the bonus I wanted, and the fact that I insisted on going to Italy to oversee my creations. After a grueling hour and a half, he agreed, and a week later I flew to Florence. The company contact met me at the airport and shepherded me to a local handbag manufacturing company

Over the next day or so I selected snakeskin and lamb leather materials, and the bag samples went from a dream into production. At one point the contact asked me if I wanted a gusset or a side or a bottom, to which I replied "I don't know" thinking he did.

The following day I was presented with a beautiful, expensive line of one-dimensional lamb leather and snakeskin envelopes. You could not get lipstick into any of them as they had no dimension. It didn't take me long to realize that the blind person who designed the handbags I had disparaged was my contact and I had been sabotaged. The following morning, he arrived at my hotel, and I led him into the lobby. I promptly gave him two choices: one I would head home the next day without samples, and tell the owner of the company what he had done. It goes without saying he would be very unhappy, because they spent a great deal of money the trip. Choice two, he could take me to the right handbag manufacturer, get the samples done and I would say nothing.

He chose correctly and I brought the samples back and proceeded to sell millions of dollars' worth my newly created line to major department and specialty stores around the country A few weeks later the other partner asked me what title I would like to have. I immediately said, Director of Design and Development.

As an added bonus I also received an override commission on the line from the dozen showrooms around the country that were selling it, so I ended up making $9000 10000 a month within the first eight weeks that I was there. This was back in the mid-80s and was a very good salary back then. Now just imagine what would have happened if I had stayed silent, in a fearbased "I can't do that" mindset, and not staked my claim to designing a better, more saleable line of handbags. I would have been sitting in the showroom making $1500 a month! Wrong choice, wrong mindset!

So, I advocate this, SAY yes instead of no. You don't know if you can do something unless you get in there and do it. Now maybe it won't work exactly right the first time, but you learn from your mistakes. When I hear people say "I'll try" I immediately rise up and sayry to pick up this pen from the desk. You don't try, you either do it or you don't. If you pick it up incorrectly and it falls to the floor, then pick it up a different way the next time, and the time after that. Eventually, you will pick it up correctly. Each time you are not successful, is a lesson in the classroom called life. You will learn what you did wrong and change it next time.

I just love the "I'll try" mindset! It is the pathetic excuse most people use rather than just do it and accept the outcome. If the outcome is not what you want, do it differently until you get the outcome you want.

The real challenge to changing the mindset for most people is pushing through the fear and risk, but you must. Without risk there is no reward. Far too many people establish boundaries which are mindsets, that they live in for most of their lives. Now loving and respecting one's family is a very important concept, however, denying yourself the freedom to soar like an eagle, to experience other cultures and countries, let these self-imposed boundaries prevent you from achieving, is not acceptable. That can occur when the fear is passed down from generation to generation which is all too common.

As luck would have it, I came from a family where fear was a large part of their narrative. This was due in part because my father was a customer's man on the floor of the New York Stock Exchange when it crashed in 1929, and he witnessed millionaires leaping from buildings or reduced to selling apples on street corners. Fear was to be a normal part of his life, and he often cautioned me not to invest in real estate or to take a risk of any kind because of his embedded fearbased mindset. Somehow, perhaps because of a left-over, rebellious attitude from my youth, I ignored the fearmongering and made my own path, meeting challenges head on and jumping off the cliff without a net or anything resembling one. I refused to accept the generational mindset that had been passed along from family member to family member. Because of that I have had some incredible, mind-blowing experiences and I urge my clients to be brave and fearless and step off the edge, replacing the fearbased mindset that is holding them back with a courageous one.

In a similar fashion I believe that in the world of relationships if it is broken and you can't fix itNEXT! You have but one life, at least as far as we know, and there are over 8 billion people on the planet. Surely there is someone out there who will love and respect you and support your goals and ambitions. If not, you are better off alone, then alone in a relationship. Trust me, there are plenty of people out there who are very alone, even though they are with another person. Frankly, there is nothing worse than that. At least alone you can do what you want when you want and achieve the dreams that another person might not support.

In the late 70s I separated from my second husband and six years later I experienced, a life-changing event, one that propelled me from a mindset of fear to fearless. People often talk about things they have never experienced with a tone of authority that is unwarranted. So, they "know" everything about China for example, but have never even been there so their "knowledge" is hearsay from the media or other similarly endowed people. When I moved alone to Africa in 2002, I had friends knowingly ask me why I was going to a place with ions and igers and ears. I had to tell them that there were no tigers or bears in Africa… but rather they were on another continent.

I had been told by a variety of these people that the Firewalk was a fake. The coals were not red hot, and the entire thing was nothing more than a stunt, if you will. Over the years I have learned that one should not give a running commentary about things they have not experienced themselves. It was interesting to note that when asked if they had done the Firewalk, or been to China or ever gone on a safari in Africa, the answer was normally a resounding no. Clearly their mindset was fear-based, a fact they had failed to deal with sopreferred to just tell others not to partake.

 So early on in life I decided not to comment on things I had not experienced personally. It was on that note that I signed up for Tony Robbins Unleash The Power Within Firewalk. It was in the San Fernando Valley at a Sheraton Hotel, and it was in the mid-80s so there were a few hundred participants, not a few thousand.

It started on a Friday night with several hours of seminar work that focused on healing the body from within, which was followed by the Firewalk. That was the start of what was to be a life-changing three-day event.

Since I was anxious to do the Firewalk, anything that stood between that and me was met with some impatience and a bit of annoyance, so the healing work we were doing seemed to be a bit of a waste of valuable Firewalking time. I had at the time a healthy, or so I thought fear of fire mindset, but would soon change that to a truly healthy, but powerful thought process rather than mindset.

The Universe works in unusual ways and contrary to my belief then, this work was to change my perceptions and my life forever. Around midnight we made our way to the parking lot area where the pathways of red hot coals stood, and people began to walk across them, albeit some with a modicum of hesitation I stood on the sidelines and argued with myself over whether I actually should walk barefoot over that path of burning redhot embers. I reasoned that no one would know, except me but at the end of the day, I was the most important person anyway. Then I watched as two little people were aided across the coals and so I marched into line. I was several people back from the front and the coals were getting darker so that made me even happier. Just as I reached the front of the line, I heard someone say, "ore hot coals," and a wheelbarrow arrived and dumped its contents right in front of me.

I had no choice but to step off repeating "cool moss" as instructed. By the time I reached the halfway mark I could feel a burning on both of my insteps. I made my way to the wet grass at the end and by that time I had made up my mind not to return the following day for the seminar. Feeling very sorry for myself and in a degree of pain I went back into the seminar to finish the night before heading home.

I arrived at my apartment at about 4:00 am exhausted and feeling sorry for myself. Big mistake as I was about to learn a life changing lesson. I pulled off my clothing and saw two fully formed clusters of blisters filled with liquid on each of my insteps, but I was far too tired to do anything about them. I put my socks back on and fell into bed vowing to keep the hair appointment I had early the next morning, but not to go back to the seminar.

I woke up a few hours later, took off my socks and to my amazement the blisters were totally healed and crusted over as if they had been there for weeks not hours. I was in shock but soon realized that the work we had done earlier in the evening to heal our bodies from within had been effective and while I had also been shown how real the Firewalk was, I learned how amazing the healing meditation had been. I couldn't wait to get to the seminar that morning and share my experience. I believe that changed my life and made me even more fearless, in a good way, than before.

Years ago I moved to Italy by myself so that I could be immersed in the experience of living somewhere International. Friends were shockedalthough not as shocked as they were when I moved to Africa alone. What was I thinking?. How could I move to Italy by myself? Did I know anyone there? Did I have any family there? Why was I doing this? they cried. What was I trying to prove?

Truthfully I didn't know anyone and had no family there or anywhere else in Europe. I wasn't really trying to prove anything to anyone. What they didn't realize at the time was that I had changed my mindset. I was alone, but not lonely and decided to go to Europe to live for a time. There was nothing more involved or sinister in my plan and so I moved, first to the outskirts of Rome, the Cassia and then to Florence. One of the things I found so fascinating during this time was that being alone I absorbed much more of each special experience than I ever had when I was with someone. Then, I was so busy trying to call my partners attention to the things I found interesting that I missed much of the actual experience.

One day I had a breakthrough. I had gone to the Vatican in Rome by myself and cried once again at the miracle of its' beauty. I thought about being there alone and how wonderful it would be to share the moment with a partner. Then the breakthrough! I thought about how my most recent ex would have dealt with this magical spot and had a realization. So often when we go with someone to a movie, a play, a place, an event, we spend an excessive amount of time sharing "our" enthusiasm and exuberance about the place or thing.. So often the person at the other end of our enthusiastic diatribe doesn't share our feelings, and we waste our experience trying to convince them how fantastic it is. There we are trying to coerce another into "seeing" what we see and we squander our experience. But now, I was empowered to sit and just absorb the magic of the moment alonebut not lonely. I looked at every brush stroke on the ceiling in a different way. A change in our mindset changes our lives and now I enjoy watching the people just be watching me. It is amusing and interesting at the same time as more often than not, the people are together but very much alone, distant, on their phones, not communicating. Normally I smile to myself and wonder if they would rather be in my shoes than their own.

Years later, before my move I ventured into the bush in Africa, alone, hiring just those people who would make my trip possible. Once again, shocked friends repeated similar concerns: "Weren't you lonely?" followed by "Weren't you afraid?"

I wasn't lonely and I wasn't afraid, most of the time that is. I was exactly where I wanted to be enjoying the magic of Africa with my Masai Guide. Hagai, who spoke perfect English and shared wonderful African stories with me. The time we spent together over the roaring campfire at night was magical as we discussed our days adventure and what was on the agenda for the following morning. I didn't compromise my needs or desires and was doing exactly what I wanted, alone but not lonely. That is an experience that you can have, being alone but not lonely and all you have to do is take it. Rememberou can be very much alone but with someone and that is my definition of lonely. Funny enough dining alone in a restaurant triggers a lot of for both women and men as they worry what others are thinking.

I had been fortunate enough to have traveled alone for business and personal reasons for many years and so I had long since conquered the fear of dining alone. There is always that initial discomfort one feels walking into a restaurant alone. My solution to that challenge was to focus on a few restaurants so that they would recognize me and greet me on my arrival. That gave me a warm and fuzzy feeling.

I am not implying that being with that special someone isn't the most magical feeling of all. But it is far better to be alone thn to be with just anyone or to be with someone who doesn't value you. This is a method to empower you to better understand and enhance your life when you are alone. Most women would rather not do something at all than do it alone. Think about how much you are missing by entertaining that thought process. You are depriving yourself of some incredible experiences. When you are on your own you can do exactly what you want when you want without compromising yourself. Alone gives you special times time to think to create to meditate to just be and reflect on who you are. You are not dependent on any other person for your life and well-being. It is simply a mindset reset.

Resetting your mindset is all about change. It is changing your old beliefs, your mindset, into new, improved ones. It is not magic but once it happens it will seem magical. You take your old unrealistic, unwarranted fears and replace them with the courage and conviction to just say yes and go for it. You erase the mindset that is preventing you from achieving and limiting your life based on the fears that are within and replace it with a mindset of courage, strength, achievement, and fearlessness.

First it is very important that you understand your values and what you truly want for your life and not just what sounds good. Far too many people ask for something in their li even though they have not thought it though. The Universe will provide you with what you desire if you focus on it and have the passion behind it, but often one focuses on something that is not what they really want and once they have achieved it, they realize too late that they were wrong. It is critical to look within and be honest with yourself about what your goals and dreams are on all fronts.

This goes for everything in your life. You must be honest with YOU first. Look deep inside and ferret out your goals and dreams and then focus on them and make them happen. Do not be fearful of change and do not be fearful of challenges

Just jump in with both feet and do it. The worst thing that can happen is thatyou have to do it again, but in a different way. There is no such thing as failure. These are merely lessons in the classroom called life. You should use these opportunities to know what to change, what to do differently, and what to repeat. It is an amazing opportunity to learn and make your life the very best one that you can.

I have built many successful businesses just by jumping in with both feet and doing it. Businesses that I had never been in before but saw an opportunity and took it. My mindset is that I can do anything that

I truly want, I just have to have the determination, passion and intent to do it. Ten years ago I went back to school to study to be a Strategic Intervention Change Coach with the renowned Tony Robbins. I also became a WHY coach, helping people find out what the right seat on the bus is for them, so they could have a more fulfilling life. Think about the anager of a busy store who spends her days dealing with customers, resolving their problems, when her true passion is to be an author, sitting alone all day writing. She may complete her job, but inside she is unhappy, stressed, angry, and impatient. This is why it is important to examine what your true calling is and how you can achieve it. Don't stay stuck in a mindset that is holding you back from the goals and dreams that you have. That said it is really critical that you look deep inside and find out what those dreams and goals really are, and don't let someone else make that decision for you. That happens far too often as family members have hopes and dreams for their children and put undue pressure on them to follow a particular pathway. You must follow your own pathway, just be certain that it is your passion and not someone else's' as that is always a trap.

Each experience I have enriches my life and the lives of those that I help to move through the fears that are stopping them. Jumping head on to challenges has led my life n a somewhat unusual pathway. My safaris in four countries in Africa have blessed me with two families in Nairobi. They both found me on a social media platform over the past decade. One is now my adopted daughter who is a teacher because I sponsored her high school. The other young man is a guide in the Masai Mara and he and his wife pay it forward big timeby getting running water for villagers who would normally put their lives in danger each day collecting water from the crocodileinfested rivers. My goal is to impact the lives of as many people as possible and I can do that with speaking engagements and my life changing coaching.

Grace C.W. Liu

GraceSOULutions
The Woman's Truth Awakener &
Professional Communication Strategist

https://www.linkedin.com/in/grace-cw-liu/
https://www.facebook.com/GraceChrysalis/
https://www.instagram.com/gracesoulutions/
https://GraceSOULutions.com
https://GraceSOULutions.com/schedule

Grace C.W. Liu, The Woman's Truth Awakener & Professional Communication Strategist, helps covertly shy and quiet women rewire their mindset, overcome self-doubt, and own their voice with confidence. As a speech-language pathologist with over 20 years of experience, she created Pearl of Grace™, a transformative approach that empowers women to speak with clarity, set boundaries, and lead with impact. Raised in a traditional Chinese household where silence was the norm, Grace deeply understands the struggle of feeling unheard. Through energy work, Human Design, and Quantum Level Reprogramming (QLR), she helps women break free from Stagnant Communication Syndrome™, embrace their worth, and communicate unapologetically. An author, speaker, and creator of the You Matter card deck, Grace is committed to empowering women to amplify their voice, step into leadership, and create lasting impact.

Breaking the Silence:
From Self-Doubt to Vocal Power

By Grace C.W. Liu

Author's Note: This chapter is dedicated to every woman who has ever silenced herself out of fear, trauma, or conditioning. As part of *Mindset Mastery: Unfunk Your Thinking, Rewire Your Brain, and Unlock Your Full Potential*, my intention is to shine a light on the mental, emotional, and energetic patterns that keep your voice stuck and your brilliance hidden.

Through my method, Quantum Level Reprogramming (QLR), and a deeper understanding of what I call Stagnant Communication Syndrome™, this chapter guides you to break free from inner barriers. This is your invitation to embrace your worth and speak from a place of grounded confidence. You won't just learn to communicate—you'll learn to liberate yourself. Mastering your mindset isn't simply about success. It's about coming home to your truth and living it out loud.

If this feels both exciting and terrifying, you're not alone. Stepping into vocal power isn't just a skill, it's a reclamation. For years, your voice may have felt like a liability: too loud, too soft, too emotional, too direct. That feedback wasn't true. It was someone else's discomfort. What you've labeled as "too much" or "not enough" might actually be your superpower in disguise.

The truth is, your voice holds multitudes. It carries grief and glory, joy and justice, wisdom and wounds. Let this chapter be your mirror. A space to recognize not just what you sound like, but who you *are* when you speak from the soul.

Here's the core message I want you to walk away with: Your voice is not a performance. It's a presence. Presence isn't about perfection. It's about being rooted, real, and ready to connect. You don't have to be loud to be powerful. You don't have to be polished to be profound.

In fact, it's often the cracked voice, the trembling hand, the raw honesty that moves mountains. Because people don't connect with perfection. They connect with truth. When you speak from your truth, you give others permission to do the same.

Let's set a new intention. This chapter isn't about changing who you are. It's about remembering who you've always been before the world told you to quiet down. Before you believed silence was safer than expression. Before you thought invisibility equaled protection.

You are not here to disappear. You are here to disrupt. To illuminate. To *liberate*.

Let your voice lead the way.

This chapter is rooted in the work I do as the creator of the Pearl of Grace™. This framework was born from my own journey and is now the foundation I use to guide other women through voice liberation, energetic healing, and identity reclamation.

You have a voice. A powerful one, carrying ideas, dreams, and purpose. Somewhere along the way, life and judgment convinced you that speaking up was dangerous. That being heard meant risking criticism. That standing tall meant being knocked down. You learned to stay quiet. You learned to shrink. You learned to overthink, second-guess yourself, and silence your thoughts before they even had the chance to leave your lips.

If you're a quiet, introverted, or covertly shy woman, this struggle is deeply familiar. It's not about being reserved. It's a constant internal tug-of-war between the urge to express yourself and the instinct to stay small. You feel unseen and misunderstood, not because you lack brilliance, but because fear whispers: "Stay safe. Stay small."

What if I told you that hesitation isn't truly yours? That the inner tug-of-war you feel isn't personal weakness, but a pattern? A symptom of something deeper, something learned over time.

I call it Stagnant Communication Syndrome. It's the mental and emotional weight of silence, learned silence, that stops you from showing up, speaking up, and stepping forward.

You weren't born afraid to speak. You were taught. Conditioned by a thousand tiny moments to believe silence was safer. Maybe it came from childhood, from family, from teachers, or from a culture that prized obedience over voice. Maybe later, you were humiliated in a meeting or ghosted after being vulnerable.

Your brain remembers these moments. And in a misguided effort to keep you safe, it says: "Stay small. Don't risk it."

This isn't your fault. You didn't choose silence; silence was handed to you through experience, conditioning, and fear. Now that you see it, you have the power to choose something different.

You're not struggling because you don't know what to say. You're struggling because something inside has convinced you that you don't deserve to be heard. That's a worthiness wound, not a vocabulary issue.

You look around and think others are more confident, more interesting, more deserving. The truth is: Your voice matters. You just haven't fully believed it yet.

Let me give you a scenario. You want to speak, to connect, maybe even to flirt, but fear creeps in. The fear of embarrassment. Of being judged. Of being dismissed. You convince yourself it's better to say nothing than risk the pain.

Rejection isn't about your value. It's about alignment. Just like a jacket that doesn't fit, it isn't a sign that your body is wrong. It's a sign to try another size.

Here's the breakthrough: You're not broken. You've just been carrying outdated programming.

And sometimes that outdated programming looks like this:

Stagnant communication is like still water—trapped, heavy, and overrun with old fears. Without flow, your voice turns murky, too. What once protected you becomes the very thing that blocks your clarity and confidence.

When you hold your voice back, it doesn't just sit idle—it festers. The same old stories replay in your mind: *I'll say the wrong thing. No one will care. I'll embarrass myself.* These thoughts become the thick algae in your mental space, clouding your ability to speak with power and purpose.

That, my dear, is what happens to your voice when fear, self-doubt, and judgment take over.

Just like stagnant water, stagnant communication builds up emotional weight. It leaves you feeling muddy, murky, and burdened by unspoken truth and unseen brilliance.

Life begins to feel like a bad rerun. The same frustrating conversations. The same misunderstandings. The same missed opportunities. It's like being trapped in a never-ending cycle where the outcome never changes.

Here's the kicker: You are not a stagnant pond. You are a flowing river. You are meant to move, to evolve, to expand. Your voice is meant to be heard, not bottled up like stale, standing water.

It's time to clear out the sludge and let your words flow freely because your voice isn't broken; it's just been blocked. You need to go deeper than surface-level tips to unblock it. Before you can start to reprogram your inner voice, you must first master your mindset. That's where Mindset Mastery comes in. It's the bridge between silence and self-expression.

What Quantum Level Reprogramming (QLR) Really Does

At the heart of it is a powerful tool I use in my work: Quantum Level Reprogramming (QLR).

Let's break it down: the problem, the fix, and the tools to help you shift.

This isn't about forcing yourself to be more confident overnight. It's not about faking it until you make it or repeating affirmations that don't sink in. It's about shifting how you see yourself, your worth, and your right to take up space.

I use Quantum Level Reprogramming (QLR) to help women like you reframe, rescript, and refresh the way they think about communication, confidence, and self-worth. It works by addressing the conscious, subconscious, and energetic levels.

Unlike surface-level tools that focus on willpower or repetition, QLR gets to the root. It clears ancestral patterns, childhood conditioning, and energetic stagnation. It doesn't just shift thoughts; it shifts identity.

I didn't design this tool. I lived it. Quantum Level Reprogramming (QLR) wasn't something I read about in theory and left on a shelf. I learned it, practiced it, and experienced its power firsthand. It became a lifeline when my own voice felt stuck. Before I ever used it with clients, I used it on myself to heal the silence I had carried for years.

Raised in a traditional Chinese household... where silence was often seen as strength and obedience, I learned early on that it was safer to keep my voice to myself. As a child, I internalized the idea that speaking up would cause conflict, draw unwanted attention, or lead to shame. Even after becoming a speech-language pathologist, I noticed I could help others find their voice but struggled to fully own mine.

And then, I became an entrepreneur. Suddenly, I wasn't just speaking to help others. I had to speak to be seen. I had to market myself, articulate what I do, explain my value, and show up online and in person. It was a whole new level of visibility, and with it came a tidal wave of self-doubt and judgment. What if people didn't understand me? What if they thought I was too much or not enough? Unlike being an employee, where structure, roles, and salaries are provided, entrepreneurship meant the spotlight was on me. If I stayed silent, no one would know who I was or how I could help. And that meant no impact and no income. The stakes felt higher because they were.

There was one particular day I remember sitting at my computer, agonizing over a social media caption. My heart raced. My palms were sweaty. I wasn't writing a speech. I was writing a single sentence introducing myself and my service. It felt monumental. It felt like the whole world would judge me for daring to say I had something worth sharing. That day, I almost deleted everything. But I posted it. Someone responded. Not with judgment but with gratitude. It landed. I realized that the risk of speaking up was far smaller than the cost of staying invisible.

It wasn't until I began doing the deeper inner work of combining mindset techniques with energy work that I started clearing the energetic imprints of those old beliefs. QLR helped with my healing journey. I wanted to share QLR with other women and to help women like me rewire not just their thinking, but the silent agreements they've made with fear. The shift wasn't immediate, but it was lasting. Now, I incorporate QLR whenever and wherever I can.

The first time I fully used QLR, I didn't even realize how much weight I'd been carrying. The resistance was strong. My mind clung tightly to old fears like they were armor. But something shifted during that session. I remember sitting in stillness afterward, not just thinking differently, but feeling different. There was space where anxiety used to be, a calm knowing that my voice was allowed.

When I spoke from that space later that week, on camera no less, something clicked. My words flowed. I felt inspired and empowered as I shared my message. People commented that it resonated with them. For the first time, I didn't just feel heard or seen, I felt validated. Fully recognized. Liberated. Like my voice finally had a place to land, and it mattered.

That moment changed everything. It wasn't a one-time fix, but a reminder that healing isn't linear; it's layered. Every time I use QLR, I peel back another layer of silence, another agreement I unknowingly made with fear. It's no longer just a tool. It's a lifeline. And that's why I share it with others because every woman deserves to feel what I felt in that moment: free, grounded, and finally home in her voice.

You've seen the roots. Now, let's rise into what's possible. Let's bring your voice forward.

Imagine this: You walk into a room. The energy shifts not because you're louder, but because you're clear. You're no longer calculating how to shrink or what version of yourself feels safest. You simply are. You speak with ease, grounded in the belief that your voice deserves space. You offer your ideas without disclaimers. You say no without guilt. You ask for what you need without apology. That's what it looks like to live as a woman who leads with her voice.

This isn't about being the loudest in the room. It's about being the truest. Confidence is not volume. It's alignment. It's the quiet strength of knowing who you are and choosing to show up anyway, even when your voice trembles.

I invite you into a gentle reflection:

What would shift if your voice led the way today? What truth is sitting on your tongue, waiting for permission to be released? What would change if you stopped asking if you were allowed to speak and simply spoke?

Take a deep breath. Now exhale with intention.

Write down one thing you wish you could say to a person, to yourself, or to the world. Then write it again, but this time, remove the apology. Remove the softening. Let it stand in its full power.

Now close your eyes and visualize this version of you. The one who speaks with conviction. Who makes eye contact. Who doesn't shrink when met with resistance. Who doesn't perform or perfect to earn love or worth.

What is she doing today? What does her body posture feel like? How does she handle challenges? What kind of people surround her? How does she speak to herself in the mirror?

See her. Be her. She's already inside you. Not a future version, but a present possibility.

If it feels too big to leap, take a small step.

Maybe that means saying *no* when you usually say *yes*. Maybe it means speaking your idea first, not waiting to see what everyone else thinks. Maybe it's writing that post, recording that video, or simply asking for what you need.

The goal isn't perfection. It's presence.

It's not about never being afraid again. It's about moving anyway. Speaking anyway. Trusting anyway.

Your voice is not a liability. It's an asset. And your story isn't too much, it's medicine.

So, here's your declaration:

"My voice is worthy. My truth is sacred. My presence is power."

Repeat it. Breathe into it. Let it guide your next word, your next choice, your next step.

This is what voice liberation looks like in real life.

Every voice you choose to use whether bold or barely above a whisper is a step toward wholeness. You don't need to become someone else to be heard. You just need to come home to yourself. And the more often you return to that inner truth, the more magnetic your presence becomes. People don't just hear you; they feel you. That's the power of an authentic voice. It changes rooms. It changes lives.

Most importantly, it changes you from the inside out. This isn't about waiting for the "right time" or being completely healed before you begin.

Small acts lead to big shifts. It starts now.

Bring your voice forward. Voice liberation begins with belief. It's sustained through embodiment. Let's anchor what you've read into your own experience.

Voice liberation begins internally, but it's sustained through practice. Let's pause and turn inward with a few soul-centered reflections to anchor your awareness.

Reflection Questions:

1. What was the first moment you remember being told to be quiet? What message did that moment leave in your body?
2. What's one thing you've wanted to say for a long time but haven't? What stops you?
3. How would it feel in your body to speak without overexplaining, defending, or diminishing?
4. If you trusted your voice completely, what conversation would you initiate today?
5. What part of your story do you still believe is "too much"? How could it become your message?

As you sit with these reflections, take a moment to shift from thought to sensation. Let's move from mental clarity to embodied awareness through a simple visualization to support your voice from the inside out.

Visualization Prompt:

Sit quietly and imagine your voice as a color. What does it look like when it's blocked? Now, breathe deeply and imagine that same color expanding. It starts in your throat, then radiates outwards into your chest, your face, your entire body. With each inhale, the color grows stronger. With each exhale, it clears old fear. Say out loud: "I give my voice permission to rise."

Once you've connected with your voice through visualization, anchor that shift by giving it language. Let these affirmations anchor what's true, and speak to them aloud or write them down to let the message settle into your body, mind, and energy.

Affirmations to Anchor Your Voice:

- My voice deserves space.
- I do not need to be perfect to be powerful.
- I release the fear of judgment and reclaim my expression.
- My silence protected me once, but now my truth sets me free.
- I speak not to prove myself, but to be myself.

Now, it's time to move your voice from intention into motion. Choose one small act today to put your truth into motion.

Pearl Practice:

- Send a message that you've been avoiding.
- Say no to something you don't have the capacity for.
- Share a truth in a conversation without cushioning it.
- Introduce yourself online or in person with pride.

- Speak one truth out loud to yourself in the mirror, even if your voice shakes.

And if hesitation still lingers, that's okay. Sometimes, the fear isn't in your present voice. It's in your past. Come back to the girl inside.

Bonus: A Whisper to Your Inner Child

Close your eyes. Picture the younger version of you, the one who wanted to speak, but was shut down. Kneel beside her. Hold her hand. Say: "You are safe now. I'm listening. You matter. And I promise, from this day forward, we will speak together."

Let these practices be your bridge. From silence to sound. From doubt to truth. From self-protection to full expression.

This is how you unfunk your thinking. This is how you unmute your life. This is your moment. Let it begin with one brave word.

Even with all this inner work, doubt still shows up. That's normal. That's human. Let me share a moment from my journey when I had to remember my own tools in real time.

I remember another moment early in my entrepreneurial journey. I had just finished a webinar. My first live teaching. My energy was buzzing with nerves and adrenaline. I stumbled over a few words. I lost my train of thought. And afterward, the replay button mocked me with every imperfection. Then an email arrived: "Thank you. That message was exactly what I needed."

That one email silenced a dozen inner critics. It reminded me that we don't have to be flawless to be impactful. We just have to be real. And real means showing up, even in the wobble.

Every time I share my story on a podcast, in a masterclass, or with a client, I reclaim more of my voice. Not because I have all the answers, but because I'm willing to be seen. Willing to be vulnerable. Willing to lead out loud.

You don't have to shout. You don't have to have a perfect pitch. You do have to say yes to yourself. To your story. To your sound.

Here's your moment. Not at some distant time when you're more ready, more healed, more perfect. Take a breath and let your voice rise.

Real power lives in the everyday. Voice liberation isn't only for big moments. It's how you show up in the small ones, too.

It's choosing to speak up in a meeting, even if your voice trembles. It's setting a boundary with a loved one, not from anger, but from self-respect. It's allowing yourself to take a pause instead of people-pleasing your way into burnout.

Voice liberation might look like correcting someone who mispronounces your name. It might look like you're initiating a tough conversation you've been avoiding. It could be asking for support, not as weakness, but as self-honoring. It could be choosing silence intentionally, not from fear, but from clarity.

Each moment you choose authenticity over approval, truth over perfection, you reclaim a part of yourself.

Here's something most people overlook: Your voice can't rise if your body doesn't feel safe. Voice work isn't just a mindset. It's nervous system work, too.

Grounding Tools to Support Your Voice:

- Place one hand over your heart, the other over your belly. Breathe slowly and deeply. Tell your body, "It's safe to speak."
- Do a gentle neck roll or hum to activate the vagus nerve, which helps regulate your voice and calm your system.
- Visualize your words flowing like a river, smooth and strong. Picture your body as the container holding that flow.

Before your next conversation, try this: Pause. Ground. Breathe. Feel your feet on the floor. Anchor into your breath. Then, speak. This is nervous system-informed voice work. It honors the wisdom of your body as much as the clarity of your mind.

Speaking your truth isn't just about this moment. It's about the ripple effect. Your voice isn't only for you. It's for those who come after you.

Think of the women in your life: daughters, nieces, clients, students, friends. What message does your voice (or silence) send them?

You are not just liberating your own voice. You're modeling what's possible for others. Let that sink in.

Every time you speak from truth, you pave the way for someone else to do the same. What do you want to be known for? What is the message you want echoing long after you've left the room?

Let your legacy be one of courage, clarity, and connection. You don't have to be a performer. You just have to be present. You don't have to have the perfect words. You just have to speak from the heart. Your voice matters. Your truth is sacred. Your presence is a gift.

Say it with me:
"I am here. I have something to say. And I am no longer afraid of being heard."

Let your story be your stand. Let your truth be your offering. Let your voice be your revolution. You are not behind. You are right on time.

Keep going. Speak on.

As we close this chapter, let's move from inspiration to integration. You've just explored layers of silence, shame, and the stories that held your voice back. You've walked through mindset, memory, and the magic of showing up.

Now, it's time to choose one bold, brave step forward. Not a leap, a small step.

Maybe that's journaling your truth today. Maybe it's speaking up in a group where you usually stay silent. Maybe it's recording a voice memo to yourself affirming your power.

Or maybe, it's sharing this chapter with another woman who needs to know she's not alone. Whatever you choose, let it come from self-honor, not pressure. This is not a to-do list. It's a path of return to yourself, your story, and your sound.

You don't have to rush. You don't have to shout. You just have to begin. Right here. Right now. You are the voice you've been waiting for. Let her rise.

If ever you forget your power, come back to this page. Reread these words. Revisit your own reflections. Remind yourself of the shifts already unfolding. You're not starting from scratch. You're returning to your soul's knowing. Because voice liberation is not a destination; it's a devotion. To the truth. To the presence. To the grace.

Keep speaking. Keep becoming. The world doesn't need another echo. It needs your truth. Let it be heard.

Don't let this be where the work ends. Let it be where it begins. Here are a few simple ways to carry your voice work forward, one intentional step at a time.

Voice Forward: Integration Tips to Keep the Momentum

1. Daily Voice Check-In: Ask yourself each morning, *Where in my life am I holding back today?* Then, choose one way to speak up, even if it's small.
2. Create a Voice Sanctuary: Designate a space: a journal, voice memo app, or quiet corner where you can express freely, without judgment.

3. Ritualize Reflection: Each week, reflect: When did I speak with truth? When did I silence myself? What do I want to try differently next time?

4. Use Anchoring Phrases: Before hard conversations, whisper to yourself, "I deserve to be heard." Let this phrase anchor your nervous system and energy.

5. Celebrate Expression: Track your wins: every text you send, every truth you say out loud, every time you say no. Witness your growth.

6. Join or Create a Brave Voice Circle: Surround yourself with others on a similar path. Whether it's a local group, a virtual community, or a few trusted friends, create a space where voices are honored and stories are shared without shame.

7. Practice Storytelling Aloud: Choose a memory and speak it aloud without censoring or editing. Notice how your voice sounds, where you hesitate, where you shine. This isn't performance. It's practice. Let the story live outside of you and transform through the telling.

8. Schedule a Monthly Voice Ritual: Set aside a specific time each month to reflect, realign, and recommit to your voice journey. Light a candle, play music that moves you, and speak your intentions aloud. Make it sacred.

Remember: Expression isn't about having all the right words. It's about showing up, practicing, and returning to your truth again and again. Your voice doesn't need to be loud to be powerful. It just needs to be yours. You don't need permission. You already have the power.

So, keep walking. Keep writing. Keep rising.
Because you are not just speaking.
You are becoming.

Stella J Tokar

CEO of B.O.L.D. Consulting™, and B.♀. L.D Women™

https://www.linkedin.com/in/stella-tokar-b-o-l-d-consulting-llc-3735b013/
https://www.facebook.com/BOLDconsultingStella
https://www.instagram.com/stella.tokar

"Whatever controls your mind has the power to dictate the outcomes of your life." - Stella's life motto

As a Neuroencoding Specialist she holds credentials from Amen University and the Neuroencoding Institute, as well as University of Miami, UVA, and other educational institutions. People remain Stella's passion and her motivation is driven by the testimony from others as they share their transforming stories of living life with purpose and power after coaching with her or experiencing one of many workshops/presentations. Others benefit from her leadership and comment on her ability to show up transparent and authentic. She has been awarded numerous recognitions in her 43 years in business, politics and faith mission, magazines, features, media, and TV host. But none is more rewarding than success in raising her 2 gown children, support to husband, Dr. Pete, and 5 grandchildren.

Just Who Do You Think You Are?

By Stella J Tokar

Years ago, I heard someone tell a story about a powerful businessman who was upset that his flight kept getting delayed. He arrogantly cut in front of a long line of passengers and rudely stated: "Do you have any idea who I am?"

Without missing a beat, the frazzled ticket agent spoke into her microphone and asked, "Attention in the terminal, we have a man at gate 12 who doesn't know who he is; is there anyone who can help?"

That's a memorable story for two reasons: First, that ticket agent was quick on her feet! Good for her. That response made a lasting impression on me. And second, how important that question is for everyone. Say it out loud, **"JUST WHO DO YOU THINK YOU ARE"?**

When have you ever been asked that question? Never? Recently?

CLOSE YOUR EYES...imagine hearing that question...

- What are you doing?
- Where are you?
- Why are you being asked the question?
- What is your response and choice of words?

Maybe you have no response at all. Finding words to answer that question takes deep thought, clarity and a true belief in yourself, right? Now, imagine this...

You are 5-6-7 years old...and parental guardians, family members are constantly asking...

"Who do you think you are? What makes you think you are so special? Why are you so different? Think you're better than we are?"

That is what I heard growing up, almost every day. I tried to fit in, but couldn't. That lifestyle just didn't make sense to me. It was like all those choices they were making, the way they spoke to each other, and activities they were involved in. I didn't fit into it, and it didn't fit inside of me. It was like trying to fit your size 7 hand into a size 5 glove. No matter how much you pull, push, grab or stretch, it just doesn't fit.

I could only show up for my life as me. I didn't know any other way to behave, dress, speak, or be. I was guarded at home to keep myself safe in an unstable environment and to save myself the grief of being mocked and bullied by my own family. But school was my sanctuary, a safe place to live out loud, my signature self.

I was convinced I was destined to live a distinct life. An alteration of the lifestyle my mother chose. My mind and heart were already stirring in wonder at what my "next" looked like. My emotions were invested in finding it. I kept rehearsing similar phrases over and over again... "This is not my life. The life I want is out there. I will find a better way to live." With no clue on how, I wondered, was determination enough?

Born to a teen mother, abandoned at birth, and later taken back by my mother when I was three years old (sounds like a movie, right?), I grew up in extreme hardship. I quickly became the "mom" in the relationship. My first stepfather became an alcoholic and a wife-beater. As a small child, I often got in the crossfire of abuse as my mother cried out for me to help her. And, I intervened every time to protect the only person I had a relationship with. After all, she did come back to claim me, right? Wasn't that love?

My mother and I found ourselves running out of the house occasionally in the middle of the night with gunfire over our heads, finding refuge at her best friend's, thinking it to be safe. What my mother never knew was that I was being violated by the man of that house. Learning mother's patterns after several days of cooling off, we would head back. My mind would brace itself in fight-or-flight mode, ever on guard to protect myself and my mother.

Just before my 10th birthday, in the early hours of the morning, while on the phone with police, yet again, I was the only witness to my stepfather shooting my mother. She ran out the front door. I heard the shot and lost sight of her. At gunpoint, he forced me to hang up the phone and locked me in my room. Only for me to hear two more shots. Can you imagine the many scenarios that were running through my mind upon hearing that commotion? The next thing I experienced was police as they broke down my bedroom door, escorted me out of the house, trying to shield me from seeing the pools of blood all over the house. I heard them saying, "She has PTSD. Put it in the report." I had no idea what that meant. The rest of the story is for another time.

With my mother no longer married to him, I finally had the space to take the next 7 years to ask myself the very question we started with…"Stella, who do you think you are?" What I started to realize is that most people don't know who they are because they don't believe in themselves. Or they attach their identity to their circumstances and wear it every day, emotionally imprisoned with no understanding of how to get out. Maybe, like my mom, they don't want to make the change. And some rely on titles, people or position for their identity.

My thoughts then began to swing in another direction, leading me to think about other questions. Like…what if I am fooling myself? Was I trying to fool others to think I was better than I really was? Did I really have what it takes to live outside that box everyone was trying to push me back into? From deep down inside me, my heart and mind were screaming back at me, almost arguing, that I was destined. But what for and what did that look like?

Many of you may be overwhelmed with the same questions, be in similar circumstances of life and/or deeply desire a direction that will lead to answers. Let me introduce you to my W.H.O.: A simple formula that got me through what seemed impossible odds. And if I can change my circumstances by changing how I think about myself and others, by golly, it will work for you also! In fact, when shared in my coaching and training, those who own it and apply it, have success. Let's get started with me revealing my W.H.O.

W – What do I need to know?
H – How do I go about it?
O – Open to change and discovery.

We all come into this world the same way. And, with few exceptions, we all start at square one in learning to walk, feed ourselves, master language, build relationships, etc. You see, at birth we are all preapproved by God, fashioned uniquely, destined with purpose. There is potential in all of us.

So, what happens along the way? Life happens!

W – WHAT DO WE NEED TO KNOW?

Although everyone is born into the same world, we all experience this world in our own unique ways. I am living proof of that. I grew up in the same household as my siblings, yet my half-brother and sister suffered issues of extreme nature. (Another story for another time.)

Why was I able to break free? My thinking. It depends on what regulates the mind. My life motto is, "Whatever controls your mind has the power to dictate the outcomes of your life" – Stella Tokar.

Be Aware of How the Brain Works

External forces flood our brains, creating a myriad of experiences, episodes that feed our memory banks. We process these memories and attach emotions to them to be stored accordingly. When the mind labels your thoughts, behavior WILL follow. How?

Thoughts ignite feelings
Feelings drive actions
Actions command behavior

The way we see ourselves, other people and our circumstances is shaped by this process. It naturally happens over and over, thousands of times per day, month after month, year after year.

At the same time, neuroplasticity is taking place in the brain, automatically, without any direction or thought from you. The brain does this all on its own and reinvents itself. Neuroplasticity is powerful, organic and its behavior is instinctive.

- The brain has the ability to change its neural networks through <u>growth</u> and reorganization.
- It reorganizes and rewires its neural connections, enabling it to adapt and function in ways that differ from its prior state.
- It responds to learning new skills, experiencing environmental changes, recovering from injuries, pregnancy, managing caloric intake, doing practice/training or adapting to sensory or cognitive deficits, psychological stress.

Important fact: the brain was created to protect you, not to set you up for success. Left on its own, it will always go to the negative, survival mode. The mind, however, is set up by you. How you process, the choice of emotions you attach to life episodes, and how you manage your thoughts all become your mindset, or better said, philosophy of your soul. And now that you know about neuroplasticity, you can use it to your advantage.

You see, we, you and I, have the power to shape the way life is viewed. You create the mind you use every day to make decisions, build relationships, think about yourself and grow. The mind is separate from the organ known as the brain.

Discovery of your identity and belief in your significance strengthens you to make better decisions and motivates you to show up in life as your best self. Those identified beliefs, a system of psychology, are used for everything thought and done. The mind will respond best to a systematic and predetermined approach. It loves to be organized and relies on patterns. This takes place in our conscious mind and subconscious. Pretty incredible, right?

Belief Begins with Truth

Without that predetermined foundation, you can be led to believe lies that the brain processes into reality. Lies that mock, bring confusion and bring constant questions of who you think you are. If you can't decipher what is true, you will believe the lies this culture hurls into your head on a daily basis! When those lies surface and resurface, instinctively you move toward self-preservation. Why? Because any emotion, healthy or unhealthy, will create like-minded action; patterns that become habits. Remember,

Thoughts ignite feelings
Feelings drive actions
Actions command behavior

Rather, you need to pause...take a deep breath, identify the emotion and execute a more informed plan of action in finding truth. Why?

- The pause gives you moments to contemplate, ask where the truth lies in all of the emotion.
- The breath rushes needed oxygen into the brain, stimulating increased memory capacity, boosting concentration, strengthening alertness, raising energy, building endurance and detoxifying.

Everyone has ANTS, automatic negative thoughts. Without pause and reflection, getting to the root will go unmanaged. Dr. Amen offers us a sure way to kill the ANT.

Identify the ANT: Call it out by name and ask, "Is it true?"
Ask: How does this ANT make me feel?
Ask: How would I feel without this ANT?
Ask: What does the shift look like?

Without a belief system that is fortified with truth, you will falter in remaining in your significance. ANTS will eat away at the memory filing system of your brain and mind, leaving you with an infestation of toxic thoughts, relationships, behaviors and no focus.

Once you make the shift to identify life without the ANT, truth wins. Truth serves as a powerful tool for change, challenging oppressive behaviors and accountability in personal, social and professional contexts.

Every time you rehearse the truth about who you are, that rehearsal embeds new patterns that the brain desperately seeks. Your rehearsal of the truth transplants the old patterns with new, healthier ones deep inside your brain and being, which is a good thing because that's where most lies go to hide. You force it out, into the spotlight, on display to be dealt with and replaced with power of truth. That mindset, or psychology, is what got me through my childhood and out of the house of lies I was raised in. In spite of them, God empowered me, and I believed in myself.

Tim Han shares a formula:

BELIEF + REPETITION = IDENTITY

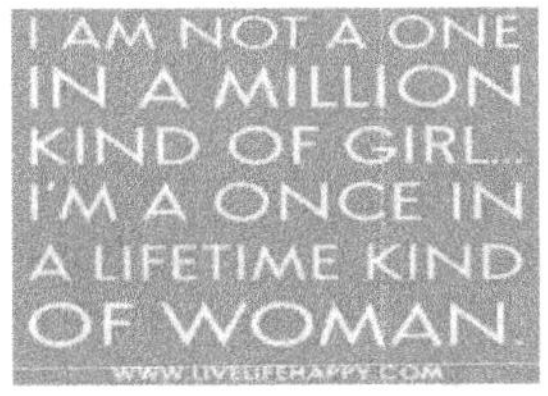

H – HOW DO I MAKE IT HAPPEN?

"Just because our battles are familiar doesn't mean they haven't transformed us!"
—Susie Larson, Author

You become an easy target the moment you stumble, and everyone stumbles. If you don't have confidence knowing you are God assigned to this earth with value and purpose, you will not reach potential. You can't sustain a fake-it-till-you-make-it philosophy.

John Maxwell says, "This fear can be rooted in a lack of alignment between what's on the inside (our thoughts and beliefs) and what's on the outside (our actions and results)."

Rewire To Refire – Practice and Repeat

It takes intentional effort, patience and tenacity to redirect your thoughts. It is all too easy to find ourselves accusing instead of taking responsibility. Anyone can feel bad on bad days. Anyone can feel good on good days.

Want to discover where to be rewired? Determine what you lack to show up for yourself. And when you face it, the revelation will bring about a powerful moment to rewire your intentions, creating space for the refire. **The brain has the ability to change, but you have the responsibility to manage the change.** So, what are you waiting for?

The belief system I built around myself gave me confidence that I would not repeat the patterns of life my mother imposed on me. So much of life is imposed. I had to rewire if I had any chance of escape.

Imposed behaviors flood your mind with all kinds of philosophies that may align with your value system or not. Make sure they're solid. If you don't have clarity and are not intentional in knowing what you value, you will be swept away into a dark vacuum.

Every day, I would rehearse, try to rewire my thinking by repeating, "This is not my life; I will find a better way to live." Making that my new truth changed my perspective deep within and planted new seeds of faith, hope and love for myself. I was not receiving it from anyone else, so I sought it on my own. This psychology I still live by set me free in ways I never dreamed possible.

Can you relate? Maybe you see yourself in a part of this process. One thing is for sure: everyone's brain works the same way, biologically. Though psychologically, everyone's mind is unique in how they process life, the many episodes experienced, and the choices presented. How will you decide to rewire?

Pre-Decide to Be Prepared

Challenge your self-narrative. What are you telling yourself in answering the question, "Who do you think you are?"

What separates you from others who achieved greatness? Did they have better schooling? More money? Never fail? Given more opportunity? Not necessarily. Those things may present an opportunity, but if taken, it is only their mindset and behaviors that will keep them on the path of greatness.

You've heard the definition of insanity...doing the same thing over and over again and expecting different results. Not going to happen, right? This only positions you with more limiting beliefs. This places you in a position of lack. When you are not all in, it costs you big time.

Adversity will force your self-narrative. If you believe you are a victim of your circumstances, you will never dare to imagine what is possible; nor will you be able to fight for victory. You play it safe and will remain stuck. You need to decide! Actually, you need to pre-decide.

Pre-decision puts you in a position of power. A planned decision will lead to a planned outcome.

As a certified Neuroencoding Specialist, I can't change the lives of others if my belief system or psychology is weak, broken or erratic. That's not authentic. I practice what I preach, and I don't teach theory; rather, proven process.

My faith dictates my value system, which gives me confidence in something proven. I lean into my beliefs that God purposely created me to live on purpose in who I am. That is the foundation of my strength. So, let me ask you, what is the source, and where do you seek your strength? For me, it's my faith. Seek deep within you; there is a value system that drives you. Discover it, challenge it.

Hardship will reveal how well prepared you are. What happens next when challenged, in difficulty, experiencing misfortune, is based on how well you prepared ahead of time. Your behaviors show up based on this foundation and will reveal who you are from the core.

O – OPEN TO CHANGE

Discover The Advantage

You've heard me say I don't teach theory. Why, because it breeds the possibility of failure and is unsustainable. Nor do I have a perfect solution. My disclaimer: Not Perfect, But Proven. It's real and works.

Change is uncomfortable for most. What you need to build into your belief is that **you are able to change.** A learned skill and put into practice, it WILL become part of your default mindset. Believe me, I know. I would not be the whole person I am today without embracing change. Simply, change is a new opportunity. When you make the shift to believing that to be true, reinvention happens...you find new "cheese". (You have to read the book on change, *Who Moved My Cheese.*)

There is a given process to change that will help you understand the stages every human person must go through in order to claim the opportunity that always follows change. It looks like this:

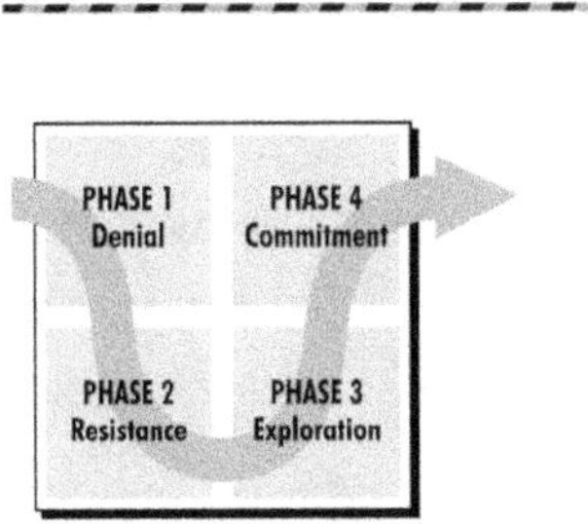

There are two steps to keeping yourself moving through the process.

1. **Stay Curious:** It will keep you open to seeing opportunity.
2. **Repeat:** Practice will create new patterns while replacing the old ones.

You must remember, it is perfectly normal to feel some doubt when making a change. Just don't get stuck. That doubt or fear is not an indication you can't make the change. It simply means you haven't experienced it yet. Make sense? It's the fear of the unknown that paralyzes so many.

To take hold of change and the growth it brings through learning, you must pass through fear and get out of your comfort zone. (You can experience the whole process in "Fear-ful or Fear-less" workshop.)

Fear can only be dealt with by facing it. Call it out! Write it down. Speak it out loud. Look at it square in the face. This works and is proven. I had to face a fear that, in my mind, I had dealt with. Here's what that looked like for me.

Opening this chapter, I shared with you the first 10 years of my life and what my household lifestyle was like. Let me fast forward the story after the shooting and police rescue.

I never told my mother that the husband of her best friend was violating me. Even as a small child, my mind and heart would collaborate in unison with the narrative that telling would only bring more heartache to my mother, so I said nothing. Over the years, I sought healing, forgave the people who hurt me and broke free of the cycle of pain and negativity. I was determined to end the many generational cycles, and I am proud I did. (Another story. 😊)

Fourteen years have passed, and I now have a family. God had vigorously been at work to restore the years of life I had lost in early life. My place in life had purpose and meaning. I was so happy.

While visiting my hometown, shopping with my mother, I saw her speaking to a couple I thought I recognized. You guessed it…it was her best friend and her husband. I immediately grabbed some clothes off the rack, ran into the dressing room with my husband running behind me, asking, "What's wrong?"

You see, up to this point, my husband was the only human being I had shared that part of my story with. No one but God knew until he knew. How could I tell him that the man who robbed me of my purity and so much more was standing feet away from us?

I fell to my knees in the dressing room, my stomach nauseous, tears came to my eyes, and I looked at myself in the mirror. I saw a face full of fear and disbelief! But why? In my head and spirit, I had forgiven. Moved on. Was happy. God had held my hand while I walked through the obscurity of that process. I was sure of it.

I sat still for a moment, took a deep breath, and let it out slowly. Then, a still, small voice from within me said, "Stella, you have to face him. You are ready for the next and final step in this journey." My mind was screaming… *W-h-a-t?? You have got to be kidding!!*

I hadn't seen this man since I was 9 years old. Wasn't forgiving him in my mind and spirit enough? I had moved on. Now, I have to face him? What was God asking of me? This was too much!

Sitting on the floor, still looking at myself in the mirror, my thoughts began to collect themselves. Coming together like a puzzle on the coffee table. Taking another deep breath, I felt I could now own my thoughts and command them to dictate a new outcome in this moment.

So, I got up, wiped off my face, and straightened my posture. Immediately, a verse came to me, and I spoke the words out loud, "Greater is He that is within me than He that is in the world" (1 John 4:4). Those words brought strength to my whole being. It pulled together my mind, heart, soul and body so that I could walk out of that room calmly, and present myself as the victor God had made me. I have come this far; I want to be all in! I knew what I had to do. I thought, *If I don't show up for my life, who will? I've got this, God! You and me!*

I exited that room, explained to my husband what had just happened, and he walked with me. I said little but managed to call him by name, so he knew I was talking to him, and got the words out, "I forgive you." Confused at hearing those words, my mother and her friend reprimanded me for being rude. But he knew what I meant. That's all that counted in that moment.

Proudly, and in controlled emotion, I walked away, thanking God with every step. My whole body was shaking, my mouth a bit dry, but my soul was soaring! I did it! It had to be a face-to-face encounter, and I immediately felt the added release. The very air I was breathing seemed purer, cleaner, as if someone had masked me with pure oxygen. I took another deep breath.

That is when I learned that even a sliver of any ANT, negative emotion that still resides within your subconscious, is toxic. It can sabotage you in a number of ways and isn't worth ignoring. It must be dealt with face-to-face, or you will regret giving it space to just be present.

You see, the power fear has over you holds you back. That's true of any ANT. And, the power over you is only as strong as you allow it to be. It will, 100%, keep you from knowing who you are and standing firm in your significance.

You must believe and practice this:

- Change is personal,   I need to change.
- Change is possible   I'm able to change.
- Change is Profitable   I'II be rewarded by change.

Merriam-Webster describes fear as "A distressing emotion aroused by impending danger, evil, pain, etc., whether the threat is **real or imagined**; the feeling or condition of being afraid."

Did you see what I saw? Real or imagined. Remember in the "W" section, I mentioned that the brain does not have the ability to know right from wrong, real from unreal, healthy from unhealthy? Negative emotions will keep your mind in a state of confusion, negativity and indecision.

Change is hard because it signifies the death of something in order to give birth to something new. Letting go…easier said than done. When in your comfort zone, you are in a deeply patterned rut, comfortable, familiar. It feels good, easy. No one is challenging you there, and you buy into the lie that you are prospering there.

One of the biggest ah-ha moments in my field of work is when people discover their brain has the ability and will to create its own realities. Since it doesn't know right from wrong, truth from lie, and loves to be right, it WILL make up what it processes to be reality.

Putting the **W.H.O.** formula to work will bring your true reality forward, and you will gain understanding that there is no long-term satisfaction or thriving in the comfort zone. To get out of and stay out of the comfort zone, you MUST pass through the fear zone. Face it.

Ask yourself...*Am I too easily satisfied with things that **don't** transform me?* Pause for a moment...think about that statement. What does a change look like for you? Feel like? Write it down. I challenge you with these extensions to the question we started with.

Leading your self-talk with "why" or "can't" only creates a voice that adds to the pain or fear source within you. Instead, change the narrative. Make declarations that dictate outcomes you can put into action.

Declare it out loud...

> **I can...**
> **I do...**
> **I am...**
> **I will...**

If you were given one decision to make that would allow you to change the rest of your life, what would it be? What would you say no to? What would it take for you to say yes?

Women don't do what they are capable of doing; instead, they rely on who they believe they are. That's how powerful your mind is in moving your beliefs into behavior. So, you better get REAL with yourself, learn this formula and these skills, and put them into practice. The real you will emerge. Put in the work and it will work for you.

It only takes one decision; one change to gain a life unlike anything you can imagine. I did it, so can you. A life that will bring clarity in purpose and answer the question we began with:

"Who do you think you are?"

"The best investment is self-investment."
– Warren Buffett

YOUR SIGNATURE   DATE

I will find my W.H.O. and I am worth it!

LET'S CONNECT TODAY.

TAKE OUR FREE BRAIN TYPE QUIZ >

Dionne Malush

Realty ONE Group Gold Standard
Owner/Entrepreneur

https://www.linkedin.com/in/dionnemalush/
https://www.facebook.com/dmalush
https://www.instagram.com/dionnerealtyonepgh/
www.DionneMalush.com
www.RealtyONEGroupGoldStandard.com

Dionne Malush is the co-owner of Realty ONE Group Gold Standard and a standout figure in Pittsburgh's real estate scene, owing much to her graphic design expertise. Since graduating from the Art Institute of Pittsburgh in 1989, she has leveraged her artistic skills to thrive professionally. Dionne's commitment to education and mentorship is evident as she prepares to become a certified Napoleon Hill instructor in 2024. She has led the Think and Grow Rich Mastermind for over six years, teaching Napoleon Hill's methods to help others achieve their potential. Her role in real estate involves mentoring emerging professionals, blending her experience with modern trends to guide them towards success. Beyond work, Dionne enjoys Pittsburgh sports, cars, and spending quality time with her husband, Jason, and her family. Her interests include traveling, boating, and snowmobiling.

Dionne is also a certified B.A.N.K IOS Trainer and a passionate student of success principles, focusing on personal mastery and educational outreach in her mastermind sessions. Her new podcast, "Shine On Success," discusses Napoleon Hill's ideas and the transformative power of adversity with various entrepreneurs. Visit www.DionneMalush.com for more information.

The Art of Getting Back Up: Building an Unbreakable Mindset and a Future You Choose

By Dionne Malush

I Was Never Meant to Color Inside the Lines

I didn't come into this world to play it safe.

Some people are born into comfort, into routines, into lives where the path is laid out neatly before them. That wasn't me. My arrival on this planet came with a silent agreement—though I didn't know it yet—that I would have to fight for space, for breath, for identity. And for fifty-seven years, I've been doing just that: carving out space in a world that rarely hands anything over without a fight. Especially to me.

I grew up in a trailer court just south of Pittsburgh, Pennsylvania—a place most people drove past without really seeing. You know the kind of place I'm talking about. People whispered about it, threw out the usual stereotypes, maybe even tightened their grip on their purse if they had to walk through it. But they didn't really understand it. And I didn't know any better. I thought this was normal.

We didn't have much, but we had each other—and sometimes, that's the only glue strong enough to hold life together. My dad was self-employed, a body man who brought Corvettes back to life with paint and precision. My mom was steel wrapped in kindness, with a sparkle in her eyes that came from her love of Christmas. She even worked as a Christmas Around the World representative, filling homes with the magic of the season which brought the love of Santa Claus into our lives.. You'd never guess it from her gentle smile, but she could weather storms that would level most people.

Their story is still one of my favorites: they met in May, married in August, and by the next spring, I was born. That's the kind of whirlwind love you can't buy in a Hallmark movie. Fifty-six years later, they were still together. That kind of commitment doesn't just shape you—it anchors you. It's like an unspoken promise that love isn't supposed to be easy, but it's worth every single fight to keep it.

The Weight of Loss Before I Could Walk

My first memory isn't of toys, birthday cakes, or carefree summer days. It's of loss.

I was just over a year old when my baby brother died at three days old. You don't understand death at that age, but you feel it. You feel the shift in the air. You feel the heaviness in the room. You feel the way grown-ups speak softer, move slower, and cry when they think you're asleep.

That grief wrapped itself around our family like fog—thick, heavy, and lingering. Even though I didn't have the words for it, I knew something had been taken from us. I learned before I could talk that love is fragile, and pain doesn't ask permission.

Looking back, that loss shaped me more than I could have ever realized at the time. It's the reason I decided never to have kids—not because I didn't love children, but because I didn't think I could survive that kind of pain again. I'd already seen the way loss can cut you to the bone and never really let you go.

Instead of building a family in the traditional sense, I poured my energy into building other things—businesses, dreams, and an armor of self-reliance.

I want you to think about this for a second:

- What's the first hard thing you remember experiencing in life?
- How did it change you—not in the moment, but years later, when you looked back?

Because here's the truth: if you look closely enough, you'll see that the hardest moments you've lived through didn't just leave scars—they also gave you tools. The question is: are you using them?

The First Battles

At fifteen, then again at eighteen, doctors found tumors in my left breast. Childhood ended abruptly. There's nothing quite like sitting in a cold, sterile room with a doctor speaking words you barely understand, but feeling in your gut that they mean trouble.

Fear wasn't just a concept anymore—it was something I could feel sitting in my chest, pressing down on my ribs. But here's what I also learned: if I could survive *that*, what couldn't I survive?

Those surgeries didn't just leave scars. They left me with a quiet, stubborn belief that no matter what came, I could get back up. And that belief would become one of the most important assets of my life.

By the time I turned eighteen, I'd already learned that life doesn't owe you fair. But I'd also learned that it will give you second chances—if you're willing to fight for them.

That same year, I attended a seminar in downtown Pittsburgh with Zig Ziglar. I walked out with my first copy of *Think and Grow Rich* by Napoleon Hill. I didn't read it right away. It sat on my shelf like a silent seed, waiting for the right time to take root. Years later, it would become the foundation for everything I teach about mindset.

Choosing My Own Way

When I graduated from art school, I knew one thing with absolute clarity: I couldn't work for someone else. I was too strong-willed, too independent, and too allergic to the idea of someone telling me what I could and couldn't do.

So at twenty-one, I did the only thing that made sense to me—I opened my first graphic design business. And on that very same day, I got arrested.

Yes, you heard that right. One minute, I was an ambitious young entrepreneur ready to take on the world; the next, I was face down on a pool table, handcuffs on, wearing a mini skirt. Not my proudest moment.

And yet... in a strange way, it was a defining one.

That day could have been the start of my downfall. Where I grew up, plenty of people let one bad decision define them for the rest of their lives. But I decided something important that day: this would not be my story.

And that's when the first pillar of my Unbreakable Mindset came into play...

Pillar One: Radical Responsibility

That arrest at twenty-one could have become the story I told myself for the rest of my life: *You're reckless. You're in trouble. You blew your chance. You are no different than the others.*

It could have been my permission slip to shrink, to settle for less, to join the chorus of "well, life just didn't work out for me." And the thing is—many people would have nodded in sympathy. They'd have told me it was understandable. They'd have said, *You did your best.*

But here's the truth about that day: I put myself there. I made the choices that led to that moment. And no matter how unfair some parts of life are, that one was on me.

Radical responsibility starts there—in the quiet, uncomfortable truth that you own your part in your own mess.

It doesn't mean blaming yourself for things you couldn't control. It means asking, *What can I control now?* It's not about fairness—it's about ownership.

The Temptation to Pass the Buck

We've all been there. The temptation to explain away a failure is strong. You tell yourself:

- *If the market hadn't crashed...*
- *If my partner had pulled their weight...*
- *If my boss had seen my potential...*
- *If my parents had supported me...*

And while those things may be true, they're also poison if you let them be the reason you stop moving forward.

When I lost my first business—a graphic design agency that I'd built from scratch to eleven employees and over $1 million in annual sales—it would have been easy to point at my business partners and say, *they ruined me.* The truth? I'd ignored red flags. I'd made decisions without enough protection. I'd trusted without verifying.

Radical responsibility doesn't mean you pretend other people didn't hurt you. It means you refuse to give them the pen to write your next chapter. And to be honest, I am forever grateful to them for the lessons. The ones that have shaped me today.

The Hospital Wake-Up Call

After the partnership collapsed, the stress hit me so hard I ended up in the emergency room thinking I was having a heart attack. My chest was tight. My hands were shaking. My teeth were chattering. I couldn't breathe right. Turns out—it was anxiety.

The doctor told me to "slow down" and "take care of myself." But here's what no one tells you: slowing down doesn't solve the problem if you're still carrying the same victim mentality. The weight you're dragging is what's killing you—not just the pace you're moving.

I walked out of that hospital with a new understanding: if my life was going to change, I had to change it. No one was coming to rescue me.

Your Power Audit

If you were in my mastermind, I'd ask you to do a Power Audit right now. Grab a piece of paper, draw two columns:

- **Column One:** Where am I blaming? Write down every situation where you're pointing the finger at someone or something else for where you are right now.
- **Column Two:** My next move. For each one, write the action you *can* take—something within your control—to shift that situation.

Here's why this matters: the moment you move something from "blame" to "next move," you reclaim the driver's seat.

When You Stop Outsourcing Your Life

When you live in blame, you're outsourcing your life. You're basically saying, *I'll wait for someone else to change before I can move forward.* That's a terrible business plan for your future.

Radical responsibility turns that on its head. It says:

- *I am the cause and the solution.*
- *I can't control everything, but I can control what I do next.*
- *I choose my response, every time.*

When you start thinking like that, you stop negotiating with your excuses. You stop waiting for perfect timing. You stop seeing yourself as the supporting character in someone else's story and start being the main character in your own.

My Dad's Lesson

My dad had this quiet way of showing us that life was ours to shape until his last breath. He didn't lecture—he just lived it. He faced every challenge head-on, and in doing so, taught me that the ending of your story is always written in your own handwriting. He didn't shy away from it.

When he died a year and a half ago, that lesson hit me harder than ever. In the months that followed, there were so many moments when I wanted to sit down and let grief take the wheel. But I could almost hear his voice, the same way I did in my toughest moments, urging me not to give up. He didn't even know until the day before he died what was wrong with him. It was heartbreaking to watch but he lived his life - his way.

And that's the heart of Radical Responsibility. It's not about pretending the pain doesn't exist. It's about deciding to stand up while you're still hurting and move anyway.

What Happens When You Commit

Here's the magic: when you commit to owning your next move completely, the universe starts responding differently. Opportunities start showing up—not because the world got easier, but because you got stronger.

In my own life, taking Radical Responsibility after losing my first business is what opened the door to real estate. That one decision— to own it, move forward, and rebuild—has since led to:

- A brokerage with over 200 agents
- A mortgage company
- Investment properties
- A podcast that connects me with world-class thinkers
- A mastermind that's changed lives for seven years straight
- Even an adorable Christmas store, Santa's Secret Shoppe

None of that would have happened if I'd sat in blame and bitterness.

Radical Responsibility Challenge:

For the next 30 days, every time something goes wrong, ask yourself: *What's my part in this? What's my next move?* Write it down. Take the action. Watch your life change.

Pillar Two: Relentless Reframing

Mindset is a meaning-making machine. Nothing in life has meaning until you give it one.

And the meaning you give it... will either chain you to the ground or launch you forward.

From "Failure" to "Redirection"

When my first business deal collapsed, I had two options:

1. **Option A:** Stamp the word "Failure" across my forehead and play small forever.
2. **Option B:** Ask a better question—*What if this isn't a setback, but a redirection?*

Some may have picked Option A. They would have curled up in the loss and replayed the injustice on repeat until bitterness was the only language they spoke. But me—thanks to Radical Responsibility—chose Option B.

That single shift in framing turned devastation into momentum. Instead of thinking, *I lost everything,* I started telling myself, *I cleared the slate for something better.*

The Science Behind Reframing

Here's why this works: your brain is hardwired to create patterns. It will look for meaning, even if the meaning isn't useful. If you tell yourself something is "the end," your brain will find evidence to support it. If you tell yourself it's "the beginning," your brain will work to prove that true instead.

In other words, reframing isn't just feel-good self-talk—it's rewiring the GPS in your head. And I believe, to this day, that if I burned the boats or lost everything I have, I'd get back up and build the next thing even better.

The Key West Turning Point

Let's rewind to 2006. I was on vacation in Key West with my husband and parents with a beautiful view, sun shining, a drink in my hand. Sounds perfect, right?

Except I knew I only had enough money to cover half of next month's bills.

That's when I discovered *The Secret*. Now, say what you will about it, but for a visual person like me, it was a lightning bolt. The core message—*what you focus on expands*—made me realize I'd been focusing almost exclusively on lack. And surprise, surprise—that's exactly what I kept getting.

So I started making vision boards. I plastered affirmations all over my walls and mirrors. I listened to *Think and Grow Rich* in the shower every morning. I didn't just dabble—I *trained* my brain like it was a muscle.

And slowly, my reality started to match my vision.

Why Reframing Isn't Denial

Some people hear "reframe" and think it means slapping a happy face sticker over a dumpster fire. That's not it.

Reframing doesn't mean pretending the hard stuff isn't real. It means choosing the *most empowering* interpretation of reality you can find.

If you get laid off, you can tell yourself:

- "I'm a failure and no one wants me." (That's one frame.)
- Or: "This is my chance to finally do what I've been afraid to start." (That's another frame.)

Both statements are "true" in the sense that you can find evidence for them. But only one of them opens doors.

The Broken Deal That Built My Career

When the partnership for my first business dissolved, I could have used that as my excuse to play small. Instead, I reframed it as a crash course in business, trust, and contracts.

That reframe freed me to step into real estate—something I might have dismissed as "not for me" if I'd still been stuck in that old narrative.

And because I reframed it as a new chapter instead of the end of the story, I entered that industry with curiosity and a willingness to learn. That openness allowed me to bring my creative skills into sales, which became my differentiator in a crowded market.

Do this enough times, and your brain starts doing it automatically.

Why Relentless Reframing Matters

The word "relentless" is intentional here. You don't just reframe once and call it a day. Life will keep throwing curveballs, and some of them will knock the wind out of you.

When my Achilles tendon ruptured 100%, I had a choice. I could focus on how trapped and useless I felt—or I could see it as a forced slowdown to notice the kindness of strangers, to learn patience, to reset.

When my dad died and my husband Jason needed a liver transplant, I could have sunk into "Why me?" Instead, I chose "Why not me? If not me, then who will carry this?" I didn't give myself a choice.

The Hidden Benefit: Emotional Agility

Relentless reframing doesn't just change your story—it makes you emotionally agile. You become the kind of person who can pivot in real-time instead of breaking when plans fall apart.

And that kind of agility is priceless in business and in life.

Reframing Challenge:
For the next week, catch yourself in the middle of a negative thought and ask: *What's a better frame?* Write it down. Say it out loud. Feel how your energy shifts.

Pillar Three: The 100-Hour Rule

Most people stop at "good enough."

They pick up a new skill, poke at it for a few hours, hit a roadblock, and then shrug.

"I guess I'm just not good at that," they say—like it's a fact carved in stone.

But here's what I've learned after decades of trial, error, and stubborn persistence:

If you dedicate just 100 focused hours to mastering a single skill, you will outperform 95% of the population in that area.

Let me say that again: **100 focused hours**—not random dabbling, not distracted multitasking, not checking your phone every three minutes. One hundred hours of intentional, deliberate practice.

It sounds simple. And it is. But almost nobody does it.

Why 100 Hours Works

Think about it. There are 8,760 hours in a year.

- If you spent just **2 hours a week** on a skill, you'd hit 100 hours in a year.
- If you went all in—**5 hours a week**—you'd get there in 20 weeks.

That's less than half a year to go from *"I have no idea what I'm doing"* to *"I'm better than most people at this."*

And in today's world, being better than most people is often enough to make you valuable, in demand, and well-paid.

My Podcast: A 100-Hour Case Study

When I launched my podcast, *Shine on Success*, I didn't know all the "right" ways to do it. I didn't have a fancy studio, a massive audience, or a production team. What I did have was a deep belief that conversations can change lives—and at that point, I needed them to change mine. I was carrying fresh grief, trying to navigate loss while still leading a business and a life. Sharing stories of resilience, mindset, and success wasn't just for the audience—it was my way of reminding myself that even in the middle of heartbreak, there's always a way forward, and someone listening might hear exactly what they needed, exactly when they needed it.

The early episodes? Far from perfect. My questions weren't as sharp, my intros were too long, and my editing skills... well, let's just say I learned a lot. But I showed up anyway.

Week after week, I hit "record." Sometimes it was with high-profile guests. Sometimes it was with local heroes. A few times it was just me and the mic, telling the truth about what it takes to keep getting back up.

Somewhere along the way, I crossed the 100-hour mark. And when I did, everything shifted:

- I stopped worrying about "how" and started focusing on the *flow* of the conversation.
- My questions went deeper because I knew how to listen for the gold in someone's answer.
- My intros became hooks instead of warm-ups.
- Guests started reaching out to *me* because they'd heard what I could do with a story.

That's what the 100-Hour Rule does—it transforms identity. I didn't just *have* a podcast anymore. I *was* a podcaster.

Why Most People Never Hit 100

Here's the truth: most people give up after the first 10 hours.

Why? Because the first 10 hours are uncomfortable. You're awkward. You make mistakes. Your brain tells you it's easier to quit than to be bad at something.

But if you can push past that discomfort—past the point where everyone else bails—you step into the zone where growth compounds. That's where skill turns into mastery.

Ask yourself right now:

- What's the **one skill** that, if I mastered it in the next 12 months, would change everything for me?
- Would it bring me more clients? More confidence? More freedom?

Write it down. Commit to 100 hours. Then reverse-engineer it: How many hours a week do I need to hit 100 this year?

The Ripple Effect of Podcasting

Here's the beautiful thing: podcasting wasn't just a skill I learned. It became a *gateway* skill.

Because I mastered interviewing, I became a better listener in business.

Because I built a consistent platform, my credibility skyrocketed.

Because I connected with guests from all walks of life, my network expanded in ways no cold email could ever achieve.

Now, I use the podcast not only to share other people's stories but also to attract opportunities, recruit talent, and open doors I didn't even know existed.

That all came from 100 focused hours.

The Discipline Multiplier

The 100-Hour Rule isn't just about the skill you're learning—it's about the discipline you're building.

That discipline becomes your multiplier. If you can stick with something for 100 hours, you can stick with the next thing, and the next, and the next.

It's how I've gone from a girl in a trailer court outside Pittsburgh to running a brokerage with 200 agents, leading masterminds, building companies, and speaking on stages. None of it came from "being lucky." It came from stacking skills, one 100-hour block at a time.

100-Hour Challenge:

1. Pick your skill.
2. Set your deadline.
3. Track every single hour you invest.
4. When you hit 100, celebrate—not because you've "arrived," but because you've built proof that you can do it again.

Loss, Legacy, and the Choice to Rise

A year and a half ago, I lost my dad.

He wasn't just my father—he was my anchor, my first love, my compass. When I was little, his voice was the one that told me I could do anything. When I was older, it was the voice that told me the truth, even when I didn't want to hear it and he still told me I could do anything. He was steady, dependable, and wise in a way that doesn't come from books—it comes from living through your own battles and coming out stronger.

And then, one day, he was gone. I remember the day before he passed, he said this, "When you get to this point and you look back to realize, this is not so bad. Go and make the best of it. I am, Dad ... for you.

My mom moved in with us around then, grieving the man she had loved for more than five decades. She was facing her pain while watching her daughters fight to hold everything together. My sisters and I have carried that loss every day since—but we're tough. We've learned how to live with the ache and still keep moving forward.

Not long after, my husband - my best friend, Jason, needed a liver transplant. It wasn't optional. It was life-or-death. And it wasn't from some lifestyle choice—Jason never drank, never smoked, never did drugs. It was a condition that had been silently shaping his future for years, and by the time we knew how bad it was, the clock was ticking fast. I knew we would have to fight hard and as prepared as I thought I was, it was even harder.

Meanwhile, I was running my company from home, managing over 200 agents, trying to keep clients happy, keep deals moving, and keep my husband alive—all while feeling like the ground was shifting under my feet every single day. Fortunately, one of our friends gave him his liver and he is doing great.

The Myth of "Strong People Don't Break"

People called me strong throughout this. They said things like:

- *I don't know how you do it.*
- *You're handling this so well.*
- *You're the strongest person I know.*
- *If anyone can get through this, it's you.*

What they didn't see were the moments behind closed doors—the tears, the exhaustion, the nights I wasn't sure I could do it again tomorrow.

And I would smile politely while thinking: *I'm not strong—I'm surviving.*

See, there's a dangerous myth out there that strong people don't break. That they just keep marching forward without ever collapsing, without ever crying in the shower, without ever sitting in their car in a parking lot because they can't bring themselves to go inside yet.

The truth? Strong people break all the time. The difference is—we decide to get back up. Every. Single. Time.

The Special Forces Perspective

My friend Zack once told me how our military's Special Forces approach loss. When a member of their team dies, they honor them in two ways:

1. They stop to grieve, fully and without shame.
2. They carry the fallen's legacy forward by living in a way that would make them proud. They honor the fallen. He told me to live honoring my dad.

That second part hit me hard. Because here's the thing—when my dad died, I had a choice:

- I could dwell in the void he left.
- Or I could live the lessons he taught me so his impact didn't end when his heartbeat did.

My Dad's Legacy in My Life

My dad believed in me.

He believed in working for yourself so no one else could tell you your worth.

He believed in taking responsibility, even when you weren't the one who messed it up.

Every time I record a podcast, every time I help an agent grow their business, every time I speak to an audience about resilience—my dad's fingerprint is on it.

The Choice to Rise

Here's what I've learned: life will knock you flat. Not once. Not twice. Over and over again. Sometimes it's a sucker punch you never saw coming. Sometimes it's a slow build of exhaustion that finally caves in.

You don't get to choose whether or not life will hit you.

But you *do* get to choose whether you stay down.

And if you're lucky, you'll realize that getting back up isn't just about you—it's about every person who ever believed in you, every person who ever sacrificed for you, every person who ever showed you the way.

Who Are You Rising For?

I want you to think right now about the people in your life—past or present—who shaped you. Who poured into you. Who gave you something you can never repay.

Maybe it's a parent, a mentor, a friend, or even someone you've never met in person but whose words or example changed you.

Write their name down.

Now ask yourself: *How can I honor them by how I live today?*

Loss as a Teacher

Here's the thing no one wants to hear: loss will be one of your greatest teachers—if you let it.

It will strip away what doesn't matter.

It will sharpen your focus on what does.

It will reveal strengths you didn't know you had.

But only if you choose to rise.

Legacy Challenge:

For the next week, wake up each morning and ask: *If the people I've lost could see me today, would they be proud of how I'm showing up?* Then live like the answer is "yes."

Where I Am Today

If you'd met me at my lowest points—after my business collapsed, after my dad died, after Jason's diagnosis and subsequent transplant—you might have thought, *She's done.* You might have believed my story was going to end right there.

But here's the thing: I've built my life on the truth that the story only ends when you stop writing it.

Today, I run a brokerage with over 200 agents who close billions in sales. I am building a mortgage company, and invested in properties. I lead a *Think and Grow Rich* mastermind that's been changing lives for seven years straight.

I host the *Shine on Success* podcast—not just as a platform to speak, but as the greatest networking and relationship-building tool I've ever had. Week after week, I sit down with people who've walked through fire and come out with wisdom worth sharing. I am more creative than I have ever been in my career since the loss of my dad. Creativity is my superpower.

And I teach mindset—not because it's a nice add-on, but because I've lived long enough to know it's the lever that moves everything else.

The Core Truth

My life is proof of this: **Your circumstances don't determine your destiny—your mindset does.**

You can come from nothing and build something extraordinary.

You can lose everything and rise again.

You can be knocked flat by life and still choose to stand.

I've seen it in my own story. I've seen it in the stories of my agents. I've seen it in the guests I've interviewed.

And I know it's possible for you.

Your Turn

If you've been knocked down—by loss, failure, heartbreak, betrayal, fear—get up. Not because it's easy. Because it's who you are.

Be the person who rises.

Be the person who rewrites the story.

Be the person who turns pain into power.

Don't wait for the perfect timing—it doesn't exist. Don't wait for someone else to save you—they're not coming. Don't wait for the fear to go away—it won't.

Move anyway.

Here's what I want you to do:

1. **Identify your fight.** What's the thing you've been avoiding because it feels too heavy, too hard, or too scary? Write it down.
2. **Choose your frame.** Ask yourself: *What's the most empowering meaning I can give this?*
3. **Commit to the hours.** Decide what skill, habit, or mindset shift will change the game for you—and give it 100 hours.
4. **Rise daily.** Each morning, get up and do one thing that moves you forward. Big or small, it doesn't matter. Just move.

The Rocky Balboa Truth

There's a line from *Rocky Balboa* that I've carried for years:

"It's not about how hard you hit. It's about how hard you can get hit and keep moving forward."

That's the whole game. Life *will* hit you hard and maybe more times that you can imagine. The question is—will you get back up?

The Invitation

I'm going to tell you something I tell my agents, my mastermind members, and my podcast audience:

The most powerful three-letter word in the English language is **ASK**.

So here's my ask for you:

Ask more of yourself.
Ask more of your future.
Ask more of the life you've been given.

Because when you do, you'll start to see just how much was always possible for you.

Now go. Move forward. And shine.

Erica Elliott

WarriorHeart Healing Hearts

Brain Code Strategist, Counselor, Speaker, and Bestselling Author

https://www.linkedin.com/in/erica-elliott-ms-lpc-b90911150
https://www.facebook.com/warriorheartxo
https://www.instagram.com/warriorheartxo
https://msha.ke/warriorheartxohttps://linktr.ee/WarriorHeartxo

I possess a Master's Degree in Counseling Psychology and have invested over three decades in my career as a Licensed Counselor, Certified Brain Health Coach, and Certified Health Integrative Medicine Professional. My expertise encompasses a broad spectrum of therapeutic approaches, such as Neurobiology, ADHD and Neurodiversity, Somatic Therapy, Energy Medicine, NLP, CBT, RET, EFT, TFT, Theology, EMDR, the Gottman Method, alongside Mindfulness and Meditation. I am an international acclaimed author, speaker and spent over a decade in the military. I am the owner of WarriorHeart Healing Hearts. As a Brain Code Strategist I champion a comprehensive healing approach to harmonizes the mind, body, and spirit. I help individuals clear up the mess to discover their MASTERPIECE using a combination of healing modalities to rapidly rewire for success! Throughout my career, I've had the privilege of helping thousands of individuals, viewing my work not merely as a profession but as a calling. I am truly passionate about empowering others to grow, heal, and soar, unlocking the incredible life that God has always envisioned for them. Having navigated my own share of trials, traumas, and triggers, I deeply understand that healing flourishes through compassionate relationships. Together, we cultivate resilience and vitality, transforming legacies. Like iron sharpening iron, if you're looking for support or just want to connect, you were destined for greatness! Be Blessed and Be a Blessing!

Clearing the Mess to Reveal the Masterpiece: How Your Brain Gets Programmed and How You Can Rewire It

By Erica Elliott

Imagine a life where you had no idea who you were, and the possibilities of becoming the amazing Masterpiece you were always created to be are merely in the strokes you place on your canvas. Just as a painter begins with a blank canvas. You were born with what psychology and education call "Tabula Rasa," the Latin word for blank slate, as was termed by the late John Locke. Blank Slate... Hmm, think for a moment what that looks like as you imagine a blank sheet of paper or clean canvas, a book with no words.

Pure Essence.

Pure Spirit.

Pure Light.

Pure Beauty.

Not a mark or a stain.

Who would you be if you were the one who wields the pen or paintbrush?

I recall the first time I heard this term. I was in a psychology class as an undergraduate. I remember reading it over and over again. The thoughts began to come: *Who would I be if I weren't raised in the place, the situations, traumas, or circumstances that I grew up in?* Who would others choose to be if they were able to wield their own pens and brushes? I was already working as a counselor, so this knowledge felt like a piece of the puzzle to helping people really heal deeply...to helping me heal deeply.

That was several decades ago, and since then, we have been able to prove a few things that create just a bit of difference from that... that you actually can have thoughts, memories, or even traumas from the womb as our brains begin laying down information in the pages of our minds even as we are in the womb.

What an incredible honor it is to sit with you here, at the beginning of a journey that could change everything. A journey into the deepest parts of your mind, emotions, body, and spirit... the Miraculous Masterpiece that is you.

As I write this, drawing from over three decades of education, psychology, brain science, counseling, spiritual discovery, and even more life experiences, my heart overflows with gratitude. Gratitude that you are here. Gratitude that you are willing to open these pages and see what else might be possible. Gratitude because I believe we all possess the power to change, grow, glow, and soar in life as the Masterpiece we were always intended to be.

Because no matter what has happened to you... No matter what patterns, trauma, self-doubt, fear, or frustration you've faced... **You are not broken. You are not too late. You are not too old. You are not too sick. You are not stuck.**

You are a Masterpiece! One that sometimes gets buried under layers of programming, pain, and confusion, but always remains, waiting to be revealed.

And now, it's time to start clearing the mess, to uncover the masterpiece that God had always intended you to be.

> *"Do not conform to the pattern of this world, but be*
> *transformed by the renewing of your mind."*
> **Romans 12:2 (NIV)**

You Were Programmed ... And It Wasn't Your Fault

From the moment you were conceived, your brain began wiring itself based on what it experienced. Though many people understand the concept of a blank page, like writing a novel or short story. I truly appreciate the computer analogy of the brain because, in truth, it is a bit more complicated than just writing a few words on a page. It truly is the constant loops and errors that come up in the mind that create us wondering if something is wrong with us. Unfortunately, it takes more than a delete button to reset the program if it's been running very long, and it all gets connected to other parts of us; even the body can hold memories, and all of these programs are charged with the electricity of emotions. Well, before I get too far ahead, let's dive a bit deeper.

By the time you were born, your developing brain had already absorbed signals about safety, connection, and stress through your mother's hormones, heartbeats, and emotions. The environment, people, resources, medical, as well as nutritional, all played an intricate part in your development in the womb. The beginning foundations of the brain and identity you would be repeating.

From infancy through early childhood, your most formative years, your brain continued wiring itself based on what you experienced through multiple facets.

Here's how your brain gets programmed:

- **Family:** How caregivers modeled love, anger, discipline, and worthiness.
- **Culture:** Community messages about identity, race, gender, success.
- **School:** Experiences with achievement, failure, acceptance, bullying.
- **Religion:** Messages about God's nature — love or fear, grace or judgment.

- **Friends and Peers:** Beliefs about belonging, betrayal, loyalty.
- **Media:** Images and messages about beauty, success, identity, ads, tragedies on the news, TV, Netflix series, and movies.
- **Social Media:** Constant validation-seeking, comparison, perfectionism.
- **Reading:** Books, Magazines, notes, letters, cards.
- **Politics and Society:** What voices are heard or silenced, ideas about power and value, both in the country you live in and in the world.
- **Tragedies:** Bicycle accident, car wreck, medical interactions, surgery, death, loss.
- **Language:** Meanings of words, tone, or emotions behind them.

Your brain absorbed all of it … like wet cement taking every footprint. By age 7, about 95% of your core beliefs were already formed.

Even more profoundly, during these early years, your brain operates primarily in the **Theta brainwave state** — a deeply absorbent, dream-like state similar to hypnosis. Everything you see, hear, and experience gets encoded directly into your subconscious without critical thinking.

You didn't *choose* these patterns.
You *inherited* them.
You *absorbed* them.

But here's the life-giving truth:
You can rewire them.

Pause here if you like, and take a deep, slow breath. Feel the truth sinking into your body. As you release the breath, knowing soon you will have the power to make changes you may never have realized were recorded that deeply.

The Biology of Programming: How Your Brain Wires Itself

Let's take a deeper look at what's happening inside your brain — the incredible, miraculous, God-designed organ that is constantly adapting based on experience.

1. The Limbic System (Emotional Processing Center)

At the heart of your emotional responses lies the limbic system, which includes:

- **Amygdala:** Your brain's alarm system, scanning for threats. When triggered, it sets off fight, flight, freeze, or fawn responses.
- **Hippocampus:** Your memory librarian, tagging experiences with emotional meaning.
- **Hypothalamus:** The command center that activates your stress hormones like cortisol when it perceives danger.

When you experience trauma — whether "big T" trauma (like abuse, violence, or war) or "small t" trauma (a friend lost their parent, or you moved schools in middle school) — your amygdala can become hypersensitive. It starts firing too often, causing even small stresses to feel like massive threats.

2. The Reticular Activating System (RAS) (Your Brain's Filter)

The RAS is a bundle of nerves at your brainstem that acts like a filter, determining what information you notice and what you ignore.

If your early programming taught you "I am unsafe" or "I am unworthy," your RAS highlights everything that confirms those beliefs.

But here's the miracle:
You can **consciously retrain** your RAS through practices like gratitude, affirmations, visualization, or CBT (Cognitive Behavioral

Therapy). As you shift your focus, your RAS starts highlighting evidence of safety, worthiness, hope, and abundance.

3. The Prefrontal Cortex (PFC) (Wise CEO of Your Brain)

The prefrontal cortex governs decision-making, social behavior, focus, and impulse control. When you are calm, your PFC leads your actions wisely. But when you are triggered, the amygdala can hijack the system — flooding your body with fear and pulling you into reactive, old programming. There is research that shows a person could be at the mall and, while inside, could not remember what they did with their keys, and if this person has a lot of hypervigilant tracks in the brain, they may immediately begin to feel unsafe in their surroundings. If a person came up to them when they were unsafe, they may see them as a threat or notice a police officer and see them as a threat. It's so interesting what can happen in the brain when we are triggered by a situation.

Strengthening the PFC through mindfulness, prayer, Meta Prayer, and reflection creates resilience. It gives you the power to pause, choose, and act based on who you *want to be,* not just who you were programmed to be.

4. The Vagus Nerve (Mind-Body Connector)

The vagus nerve is a long nerve connecting your brainstem to your heart, lungs, gut, and more. It plays a huge role in regulating emotions, digestion, immune response, and your overall sense of safety.

When you feel secure and loved, your vagus nerve functions optimally. When you feel chronic stress, it gets dysregulated — leading to anxiety, depression, digestive issues, immune problems, tension in the body, and so much more.

Healing your vagus nerve through:

- Deep Breathing and Breath Work

- Singing or humming
- Prayer and Meta Prayer
- Cold exposure or an ice cube to the base of the skull
- Laughter
- Gentle Somatic Movement
- Tapping
- EMDR
- Exercise – Yoga, Tia Chi, Qi Gong, Running
- Hyperbaric Treatments

...can powerfully rewire your nervous system for safety and peace.

5. Mirror Neurons (Social Learning and Emotional Contagion)

Mirror neurons allow you to "catch" the emotions of people around you.

If you grew up around fear, anger, or instability, your mirror neurons wired those patterns into your body and mind. For some individuals, you may mimic those patterns, while others mimic patterns completely opposite for a variety of reasons. Or you may mimic one caregiver versus the other if you lived in a home where one exhibited the behavior you tend to exhibit. Example: if a parent or caregiver yelled at you… You may adopt the yelling, or you may adopt the freeze or anxious response every time you hear yelling. But healing is possible when you begin surrounding yourself with safe, loving, emotionally regulated people.

Relationships can hurt —
but relationships can also heal.

Reflection Question: As you read about your brain's wiring, what part resonated most with you? Where do you feel hope stirring? When we are able to identify the behavior and where it came from, it helps us to release it more easily.

You Were Wired for Survival — But Created for Thriving

Your brain's primary job is to **keep you alive**, not necessarily to make you happy.

Old programming — even if it's self-sabotaging, limiting, or painful — exists because, at one point, it helped you survive.

For example:

- Shutting down emotionally to avoid feeling rejection.
- Staying small to avoid drawing attention and potential danger.
- People-pleasing to stay connected to caregivers.
- Anxiety when an attached person leaves you or returns.

These survival patterns *worked* — until they didn't.
Because you were made for more than just surviving.

You were created for **thriving**.

Thanks to **neuroplasticity** — the brain's miraculous ability to create new neural connections at any age — you are never stuck.

Every prayer, every positive thought, every small new action creates fresh neural pathways. Over time, the old survival patterns weaken, and new thriving patterns grow stronger. However, it does take work, and you also need to understand how to rewire quicker. Just seeing a pattern doesn't make it change; however, that is the first step to change.

You are literally **renewing your mind** and **rewiring your brain** in real time.

Triggers Are Invitations, Not Condemnations

Old wounds leave old neural tracks.
When a trigger happens — a memory, a comment, a situation — your brain lights up old wiring.

That does **not** mean you're broken.
It simply means your brain found a familiar path.

Healing looks like:

- **Noticing** the trigger without judgment.
- **Pausing** before reacting.
- **Allowing** a feeling without judgement.
- **Choosing** a micro-shift: a breath, a prayer, a gentle redirect.
- **Repeating** these micro-shifts over and over, strengthening the new path.

Relapses are normal.
Regression is normal.
Healing is non-linear.

Each trigger is not a failure — it's an invitation to rewire.

I encourage my clients to pause and take a breath whenever something feels off. Not just any breath — but one that gently lands in the center of the chest, the heart space. It's a simple but powerful practice that helps shift the nervous system and opens a window of clarity. In that pause, we give ourselves a chance to observe rather than react.

Our emotions are not the enemy — they're messengers, but we have to pause to understand what the emotions are telling us. Like a spiritual GPS or an internal compass, emotions give us information about what's aligned or misaligned with our core needs, beliefs, and boundaries. They're not meant to be feared or ignored but understood.

Here's the catch, though: our brains are wired to replay what feels familiar. When something upsetting happens, we tend to ruminate on it — reliving the moment in our minds, retelling it to others, reinforcing the same neural pathways every time we do. And the more we rehearse it, the deeper that groove becomes in the brain.

This is how emotional pain becomes programmed.

But here's something most people don't realize sometimes: what we're reacting to isn't really about the present moment. It might be a current situation that feels eerily similar to something painful from the past. It could be an old wound from childhood, a moment when we felt invisible, shamed, or afraid — or a memory from a toxic relationship that never truly healed. And suddenly, the body and brain light up as if it's happening all over again. That's not because you are not intelligent or broken; it's just a programming and can be very unconsciously driven until we learn to take a pause and check it out.

This is where mindful awareness changes everything. When we can pause and notice the emotion — not suppress it or judge it but truly acknowledge it — we open the door to healing. Breathing into the sensation, we give it room to move and shift. Then, we ask ourselves: *Is this pain from now, or is it echoing from somewhere else?*

By recognizing the difference, we reclaim our power. We stop projecting past hurts onto present people. We shift from surviving old patterns to consciously choosing how we want to respond. That's the beginning of rewiring.

And just as rehearsing painful experiences wires the brain toward fear and self-protection, rehearsing the good — *on purpose* — builds new neural connections that lead us toward joy, safety, and trust. When something kind or beautiful happens, linger there. Breathe it in. Feel it. Tell yourself the story of that moment again and again, not out of denial, but because your brain needs repetition to make the good stuff stick.

This is where mindfulness becomes medicine. When we stay present with the positives, practice gratitude, and intentionally reflect on moments of peace or connection, we are literally building new pathways in the brain. It's not magic — it's neuroplasticity. And it's available to you every single day.

"I praise you because I am fearfully and wonderfully made; Your works are wonderful, I know that fully well."
Psalm 139:14 (NIV)

The Power of Prayer and Meta Prayer on the Brain

Prayer is not just spiritual — it's deeply biological.

Brain scans show that prayer — especially meditative, heartfelt prayer — lights up the **anterior cingulate cortex** (associated with compassion and connection), strengthens the **prefrontal cortex** (wise decision-making), and calms the **amygdala** (fear center).

Meta Prayer — praying compassionately for yourself and others — enhances empathy circuits, reduces self-judgment, and increases emotional resilience.

Simple Meta Prayer Practice:

1. Picture yourself with tenderness in the state of uneasiness or trigger.
2. Whisper (or think): "May I feel love. May I feel peace. May I feel hope." (Do this three times.)
3. Picture someone you struggle with.
4. Whisper: "May you feel love. May you feel peace. May you feel hope."
5. Alternate between yourself and others.
6. End by inviting God's love to surround you both.

Practicing Meta Prayer daily:

- Strengthens your vagus nerve in a healing way to oscillate from one feeling to another in safety.
- Lowers cortisol.
- Deepens your brain's wiring for love, compassion, and resilience.

Prayer changes the brain.
Prayer renews the mind.
Prayer heals the heart and body.

Reflection Question: How could you begin making prayer and Meta Prayer a part of your daily rewiring practice?

If you are enjoying this book and ready to learn how to reprogram your brain for manifesting an abundantly blessed life more easily, you will want to check out the book ***Breath of Heaven Manifesting God's Way, using the Laws of the Bible and Brain Science to create an Abundantly Blessed Life.*** It's a book that is packed full of evidence-based tools to retrain your brain and clear blocks to blessings.

Practical Tools to Begin Rewiring Your Mind, Body, and Spirit

Rewiring your brain isn't about giant leaps.

It's about consistent, small, daily practices that send your brain the message:

"It's safe to change. It's safe to heal. It's safe to thrive."

Here are some of the most powerful brain-and-spirit tools you can start using immediately:

Gratitude Practice

Gratitude isn't just an attitude — it's a *rewiring tool.*

When you list things you're grateful for, you shift your Reticular Activating System (RAS) to scan for blessings instead of dangers.

Exercise:

Every morning or evening, write 3–5 specific things you are grateful for.

Feel the gratitude in your body — let it warm your chest, your belly, your mind.

This feeling "burns" new wiring into your brain.

16 Positives to Shift

When someone comes to me feeling stuck — whether it's in a relationship, with their job, or even with themselves — I gently guide them into a simple but powerful exercise. I ask them to write down at least **16 positive things**. Sixteen might sound like a lot at first, but it's intentional. Whether it's about themselves, the person they're struggling with, or the situation at hand, this practice starts to gently shift the mental and emotional atmosphere.

You see, neuroscience tells us that it takes about **16 seconds of focused attention on something positive** to begin rewiring the brain and move from a stress or fear response toward a more balanced, neutral, or even hopeful state. That's why I started using the "16 Positives" practice for the areas in life where people feel the most emotionally tangled. And let me tell you — it works.

If you're upset with your partner, your child, your coworker, or even your own reflection in the mirror, I challenge you: pause, take a breath, and sit down with a piece of paper. Then write out 16 things you genuinely appreciate or respect about that person — or about yourself. They don't have to be huge. Even small truths like "They have a great laugh" or "They always bring the trash cans in without being asked" count.

Why? Because **where your focus goes, your energy flows**. If you keep ruminating on what's wrong, your brain will wire more deeply into irritation, resentment, and disconnection. But if you shift your attention — even briefly — to what is good, right, or simply human in the situation, your neural pathways start to reroute. You begin to soften. You begin to see.

This is also a great tool for breaking free from obsessive loops in your thinking. When your mind keeps replaying the same frustrating thought over and over, the "16 Positives" exercise interrupts the pattern. It invites you to redirect your mental energy with intention — and the brain responds beautifully to intentionality.

Give it a try. The next time your thoughts spiral or your heart feels heavy, reach for your pen instead of your anger. Your brain is waiting for a new pattern — and you have the power to create it.

Breathwork and Vagus Nerve Healing

Deep belly breathing:

- Stimulates the vagus nerve to bring it into a peaceful state.
- Calms the amygdala.
- Strengthens the prefrontal cortex.

Exercise: 4/7/8 (Dr. Andrew Wiel has a lot of great information on 4/7/8 breathing)

- Inhale deeply for 4 counts.
- Hold for 7 counts.
- Exhale slowly for 8 counts.
- Repeat 4 times.

Breathing like this releases the neurochemical GABA in the brain, which makes you feel calmer. It also sends your brain the signal: **"I am safe now."**

I often encourage my clients to even say words like **"I am safe"** when they do this exercise to also rewire the brain more deeply. When we use multiple senses, we rewire more quickly.

Visualization: Seeing Your Healed Self

When you visualize a goal or healing, your brain lights up the *same* pathways as if it's happening in real life.

Neuroscience proves that *rehearsal of success* strengthens the brain's belief in it.

Visualization Exercise:

- Close your eyes.
- Imagine yourself fully healed — emotionally, physically, mentally, and spiritually.
- Imagine what you see, hear, smell, taste, and touch.
- Let yourself feel the peace, joy, and gratitude of your healed state.
- Anchor it with prayer: "Lord, thank you for completing the good work you began in me. By Christ, I'm healed."

Even just 5 minutes a day powerfully rewires your mind toward healing, especially when you add your five senses. I have so many clients who have shifted some of the most difficult stuck areas in their lives by adding the visualization tool regularly to rewire the brain.

Micro-Steps

Big goals often feel overwhelming.

Your brain craves **small, doable steps**.

Each time you succeed at a tiny action, dopamine is released, strengthening new pathways.

Exercise:

Choose to set your day up with Micro-Steps. Instead of focusing on doing something for an hour, set a timer for 15 or 20 minutes, then take a pause, get up and stretch, and see what happens. Make a list and prioritize it, asking yourself what is one task that, by completing it, makes you feel better or gets you closer to your goal. Use that as the task you work on first, but work on it using micro-times. There is plenty of research that shows when we do tasks in smaller increments and then take a break, stretch, and breathe, our brains actually work better.

Consistency beats intensity.

After I had a major health crash plus a brain injury, I couldn't do things at the same level. The Micro-Steps were a lifesaver. I also have ADHD, and time chunking has always been helpful, but truthfully, the Micro-Steps have been a game-changer, and I still use them often.

Somatic Work: Healing the Body-Mind

Old trauma isn't just in your mind — it's stored in your body.

Somatic (body-based) healing helps clear trauma imprints, regulate your nervous system, and stabilize emotions.

Simple somatic practices: First, notice how you feel and where you feel it in the body, then do some of the following exercises as you breathe out of those places gently, lovingly, peacefully.

- Gentle stretching
- EFT tapping (emotional freedom technique)
- Dancing to music you love
- Self-hugging or rocking
- Walking barefoot on grass (grounding)

The body keeps score —
but the body can also **reset**.

It's really great if you can name the emotion. For example, "I feel fear in my chest," or "I feel anxiety in my stomach." Say words like "I allow myself to feel anxiety, even though I don't want to feel anxiety," as you move and breathe it out. It can be so powerful.

Healing Attachment Wounds

Much of your early programming came through relationships.

Healing includes:

- Safe, consistent relationships now with healthy boundaries on toxic individuals.
- Inner child work: nurturing yourself with the love you needed.
- Somatic regulation: helping your body feel safe.
- God's unconditional love: daily immersing yourself in His truth.

You are not too damaged.
You are not too late.
You are still loveable, still worthy, still repairable.

One exercise I love to do with individuals is to see a young version of yourself and love that image of you (hug, hold, rock) as if you would your own child or niece/nephew until the child feels peaceful. I have some exercises in my inner child courses that walk you through this.

I can't tell you how many people have reported amazing shifts in their lives and in their relationships by adding this tool.

Real-Life Example: Clearing the Mess, Revealing the Masterpiece

I once worked with a woman named Claire (name changed for privacy) who struggled with overwhelming anxiety, people-pleasing, and a deep fear of failure. Every success in her life came with a flood of self-doubt and shame.

When we began working together, Claire learned something powerful:

Her brain wasn't *broken.*

It was *programmed.*

Her early home had been filled with criticism, perfectionism, and emotional withdrawal. Her mirror neurons had absorbed the belief that she was "never enough." Her RAS filtered the world to find proof of her failures. Her amygdala fired at the slightest hint of rejection.

At first, Claire felt hopeless — as if this was "just who she was."

But as she started small rewiring steps:

- Gratitude journaling to shift her RAS
- Deep breathing to regulate her vagus nerve
- Visualization of her confident, loved self
- Inner child work, loving the young her
- Meta Prayer to soften judgment toward herself and others
- Scripture meditation to renew her identity

...something miraculous began happening.

The old pathways didn't disappear overnight. Triggers still came. Tears still came.

But **now she had tools.**

She understood what was happening inside her brain and body — and she had the power to respond differently.

Month by month, Claire's self-criticism weakened. Her prefrontal cortex strengthened. Her nervous system calmed. Her joy grew.

Today, Claire walks with confidence she once thought was impossible.

Not because her life got easier — but because her brain and spirit got stronger.

She didn't erase the old programming overnight.

She simply kept choosing her healing, again and again and again. Little by little, she healed, rewired, and now she rarely gets dysregulated, and if she does, she moves through it quickly to peace. She now lives a healthy, abundantly blessed life as the Masterpiece she was always created to be.

And so can you.

> *"For we are God's masterpiece. He has created us anew in Christ Jesus, so we can do the good things he planned for us long ago."*
> **Ephesians 2:10 (NLT)**

Final Reflections: You Were Always Meant to Heal

Healing is not about perfection.

It's about returning to love — again and again.

Clearing the mess is not about erasing your past.

It's about letting God reframe it — turning ashes into beauty, mourning into dancing.

Neuroscience proves you are rewiring your brain all of the time, every day.

Scripture promises you are being transformed by the renewing of your mind.

You were never too damaged.
You were never too late.
You were never too far gone.

You are a masterpiece, already placed inside you by a loving Creator and just waiting to be revealed.

And today, your healing begins.

You're ready.

Let's begin.

Proverbs 23:7 (KJV):
"For as he thinketh in his heart, so is he..."

I pray this book has blessed you and that you use and share the tools you've learned. I have a book that expands these areas and so much more that will be released in November of 2025 called ***We Repeat What We Don't Rewire – It's a Program.*** If you found this book helpful, may I ask you a favor? Please leave a review on Amazon. Thank you!

As a Brain Code Strategist, I help people rewire with evidence-based tools to rapidly clear the mess and transform your life into the successful Masterpiece you were always created to be! People also love me speaking to their groups and organizations, teaching them tools in a fun, interactive way. I'm excited to connect, and you can find free resources on the link below. I am always adding new tools and links. Be Blessed and Be a Blessing!

Lovely LaGuerre

Founder and CEO of Pure Heavenly Hair, LLC

https://www.linkedin.com/in/lovelylaguerre
http://facebook.com/pureheavenlyhairboutique
https://www.instagram.com/lovelyvegascommerciallv
www.LovelySellsVegas.com
www.PureHeavenlyHair.cominstagram.com/pureheavenlyhair

Lovely LaGuerre is a powerhouse in the world of entrepreneurship an acclaimed Wealth Creator, Commercial and Luxury Real Estate, Amazon Best Time Seller, and International Bestselling Author. With a passion rooted in transformation and empowerment, she's become a beacon for women and leaders seeking to elevate their lives and businesses with authenticity, grace, and strategy. Lovely LaGuerre is a visionary real estate professional, committed to guiding people to financial freedom through real estate investing. Having a strong passion for real estate, she believes that "the best investment on Earth is Earth." Her areas of expertise include commercial and luxury real estate, wealth creation strategies, and market flexibility. She combines business sense with empowering others, which makes her an industry trailblazer. A transformational consultant and dynamic speaker, Lovely empowers individuals to unlock their fullest potential while thriving in both life and business. She combines deep industry expertise with heartfelt guidance, helping others lead boldly, create wealth intentionally, and make a lasting impact. As the visionary founder of Pure Heavenly Hair and Beauty Boutique, Lovely has redefined luxury in the beauty space. Her brand bridges the gap between opulence and accessibility, offering premium wigs and an exclusive cosmetic line tailored for modern professionals, go-getters, and beauty lovers alike. Her business isn't just about products it's a celebration of confidence, culture, and self-expression. "The path to success varies for each individual. However, becoming a true successful leader requires unwavering commitment, wholehearted dedication, and the ability to acknowledge and celebrate the success of others."

Lead with Vision, Grow with Discipline: My Blueprint for Lasting Success

By Lovely LaGuerre

Identity and Mission

My name is Lovely LaGuerre. I am a master of the growth mindset, a builder of vision, and a believer in the power of persistence. My life's work is to lead with clarity, create with purpose, and inspire others to rise above limitations.

I have built my businesses and my brand with the belief that leadership is not about a title. It is about influence, consistency, and the courage to think forward when the path ahead is unclear. I have faced moments where the easy answer was to stop. I chose to move forward. I chose to grow.

From the start, I have been intentional about my mission to guide people into their own strength, to help them see that their potential is not fixed. Your mind is a tool. When you train it to see possibilities instead of obstacles, you start shaping your future instead of waiting for it.

Growth is not only a mindset. It is a daily choice.

Early Entrepreneurial Vision

When I first stepped into entrepreneurship, I knew my journey would not be simple. I had no illusions that success would fall into my lap. My advantage was my mindset. I understood that skills could be learned, strategies could be tested, and setbacks could be studied until they became stepping stones.

I started in industries where competition was high and expectations were higher. Luxury beauty. Commercial real estate. Business consulting. Each space demanded more than technical knowledge. It demanded the ability to adapt quickly, lead decisively, and communicate with conviction.

I watched others wait for perfect timing. I learned early that waiting often meant missing the moment. My vision was never about taking reckless risks. It was about taking informed, decisive action while others hesitated.

First Major Business Challenge

One of my first major challenges was building a brand in a crowded market. When I launched Pure Heavenly Hair and Beauty, I was entering a field filled with established names. Consumers had options, and loyalty was hard to earn. The problem was not whether I had a quality product. The problem was standing out without compromising my values.

Many business owners in this space compete on price, cutting corners to attract short-term sales. That was never my approach. I refused to lower my standards to win attention. My challenge was to communicate the value behind my products in a way that connected with my audience's emotions and priorities.

Breakthrough Strategy

I built my brand on experience, not only on transactions. Every purchase became a relationship. I focused on exceptional customer interactions, personalized service, and product excellence. I told the story behind the products where they came from, why they were created, and how they served the customer's lifestyle.

This strategy worked because people connect with people, not faceless companies. Within months, my client retention rate was higher than the industry average. Word-of-mouth referrals became my strongest marketing tool. I learned that value is not what you claim; it is what others confirm through their experience with you.

Lessons on Leadership

That early challenge shaped my leadership philosophy. Leading a business means leading yourself first. You cannot expect others to believe in you if you do not have discipline, resilience, and focus. I learned to set clear priorities, to make decisions based on data and values, and to keep my word to myself.

Leadership is not about doing everything. It is about knowing what matters most and protecting it from distraction. When I built teams, I looked for people who shared that focus. I did not want followers. I wanted contributors who brought their own strengths to the table.

Scaling and Innovation

As my businesses grew, so did the complexity of decisions. Scaling is not only about increasing sales. It is about building systems that sustain growth without sacrificing quality. I invested in training, technology, and partnerships that aligned with my standards.

In real estate, I moved from small transactions to high-value deals in the luxury and commercial sectors. This shift required sharper negotiation skills, deeper market analysis, and stronger networks. I learned that high-value clients expect more than results; they expect discretion, expertise, and solutions before problems appear.

The Mindset Shifts That Changed Everything

Three mindset shifts transformed my results.

First, I learned to see problems as opportunities to refine my approach. Every challenge holds data about what works and what does not.

Second, I trained myself to think in terms of long-term impact instead of short-term wins. This kept me from making desperate moves that could weaken my foundation.

Third, I committed to constant learning. I read, studied, sought mentorship, and tested new methods. I did not wait until something failed to look for a better way.

Second Major Business Challenge

A larger challenge came during a market downturn. Consumer spending slowed, real estate deals stalled, and competition intensified. Businesses were closing around me. I had to decide whether to reduce operations or to adapt faster than the market shifted.

I chose to adapt. I restructured my business offers to meet the changing needs of clients. In real estate, I shifted focus toward investors looking for long-term value in a slower market. In beauty, I emphasized products that provided lasting quality over temporary trends.

The Discipline of Daily Actions

Growth is not a single decision. It is the accumulation of consistent, intentional actions. I learned early that how you spend your day is how you build your future. Success rarely comes from grand gestures; it comes from doing the small, critical things over and over until they become second nature.

My daily routine is simple but deliberate. I start with my priorities written the night before. I dedicate my first hours to the most important work, not the most urgent. I limit distractions. I keep meetings short and purposeful. I protect time for thinking, planning, and reviewing progress.

This discipline ensures I am leading my business instead of reacting to it. I do not let email, messages, or demands from others dictate my focus. I control my attention, and that control allows me to make better decisions.

Building Alongside My Teams

No leader succeeds alone. The strength of your team reflects the strength of your leadership. I have built teams in beauty, real estate, and consulting. In every case, my hiring decisions focused on character first and skill second. Skills can be taught; values are harder to change.

I create clarity from the start. Each person knows their role, their goals, and the standards they are expected to uphold. I encourage independent thinking, but I also expect accountability. I have no interest in micromanaging. My goal is to develop leaders within my organization, not followers waiting for instructions.

One of the most valuable lessons I have learned about teams is that culture beats strategy when the pressure rises. A team that trusts each other, shares a clear mission, and feels ownership over results will outperform a team that is technically skilled but disconnected.

Decision-Making Under Pressure

Every entrepreneur will face moments where a decision must be made without full certainty. The ability to decide quickly, with limited information, separates those who advance from those who stall.

I follow a process. I define the problem in one clear sentence. I gather the most relevant facts I can within a set time frame. I list the possible options and weigh their potential impact. Then I decide and commit.

I do not waste energy on what-ifs once a decision is made. My focus shifts to execution. If the choice turns out to be wrong, I correct course quickly. Indecision costs more than a wrong decision followed by fast adjustment.

Understanding Your Market Better Than Anyone

In both beauty and real estate, my competitive edge has been deep market knowledge. I know what my clients want before they say it. I study buying trends, consumer behavior, and economic signals. I track my competitors but focus more on serving my clients better than they do.

When I launched new beauty products, I did not guess what would sell. I spoke with customers, reviewed their buying history, and observed how they interacted with products online. In real estate, I anticipate shifts in demand by staying informed on population growth, job creation, and development plans in the areas I serve.

Your market will tell you everything if you listen. Too many entrepreneurs guess instead of measure. Data does not lie, and when you combine it with insight, you can position yourself ahead of the curve.

Adapting to Changing Conditions

Change is constant. Markets evolve, consumer habits shift, technology advances, and unexpected events disrupt plans. I do not fear change; I prepare for it.

During times of uncertainty, I increase communication with my clients and my team. I focus on what remains in my control my effort, my service quality, my ability to connect with people. I adjust offers to fit the current climate without abandoning my long-term goals.

In one year, I had to restructure an entire marketing plan for my beauty brand when supply chain issues slowed deliveries. Instead of waiting for problems to pass, I introduced new product bundles that maximized available inventory and kept customers engaged. That decision helped strengthened customer loyalty.

Lessons From Setbacks

Every setback has taught me something valuable. When a real estate deal collapsed after months of preparation, I examined the process to identify weak points. I realized that one missing contract clause could have prevented the loss. That mistake never happened again.

When a product launch underperformed, I did not blame the market. I reviewed the messaging, the timing, and the distribution channels. The next launch exceeded projections because I corrected what I had learned.

The lesson is simple: take full responsibility. The moment you start blaming external factors, you lose the ability to control your outcome.

Leading With Transparency

People respect honesty, especially in business. I share the truth with my clients, my team, and my partners. If there is a delay, I inform them immediately and explain the solution in place. If a goal is at risk, I discuss what needs to change to get back on track.

Transparency builds trust, and trust is a long-term asset. Many of my clients have stayed with me for years because they know I will never hide problems or make promises I cannot keep. In luxury markets and high-value transactions, trust is currency.

Creating Value That Lasts

The most successful businesses focus on creating value, not chasing sales. Sales follow value. My goal is always to leave the client better off than before they met me, whether they buy once or a hundred times.

In beauty, that means products that improve confidence and performance, not temporary fixes. In real estate, that means properties that appreciate over time and meet the client's needs for years. In consulting, that means strategies that work even after I am no longer advising.

When you think in terms of value, your decisions shift. You invest in quality over quantity. You focus on relationships over transactions. And you build a reputation that attracts clients without constant chasing.

Mentoring the Next Generation of Leaders

One of the most fulfilling parts of my work is mentoring other entrepreneurs, especially women. I know what it feels like to start with a vision but limited guidance. I share my knowledge so others can accelerate their path and avoid costly mistakes.

I consulted them on how to position themselves and negotiate with confidence, and how to maintain their mental resilience during difficult seasons. I remind them that leadership is not a performance for others; it is a commitment to yourself and those you serve.

Protecting Your Energy and Focus

Sustained success requires energy management. You cannot lead effectively if you are depleted. I protect my energy by setting boundaries around my time, limiting negative influences, and keeping my goals visible every day.

I schedule recovery time the same way I schedule meetings. I make space for family, friends, and personal growth. This balance keeps me sharp in business and grounded in life.

Burnout is not a badge of honor. It is a warning sign. Leaders who ignore it lose clarity and make poor decisions. Protecting your energy is protecting your business.

Expanding the Vision

I am not interested in building one successful business and stopping. My vision extends into multiple industries and markets. I believe in building structures that create opportunities for others.

In the next decade, I will expand my beauty brand internationally, develop more real estate projects that transform communities, and create training programs that equip entrepreneurs with the skills they need to compete globally.

Expansion is not about ego. It is about impact. The larger the platform, the greater the reach of the message and the resources.

Advice to Emerging Leaders

For those who are starting their leadership journey, I offer this advice:

1. Decide your mission before you decide your method.
2. Stay consistent when progress feels slow.
3. Keep learning even after you achieve your first goals.
4. Surround yourself with people who challenge you to grow.
5. Build systems that work without you.
6. Measure results, not activity.
7. Treat every person you meet as a potential partner, not a transaction.

Leadership is not about having all the answers. It is about asking better questions and acting with courage in the face of uncertainty.

The Legacy I Am Building

My legacy will not be defined by sales numbers or awards, though I am proud of them. It will be defined by the people whose lives were better because they crossed paths with my work.

I want to be remembered as a leader who made growth accessible, who showed others that mindset is the foundation for every success, and who proved that you can lead with integrity and still achieve extraordinary results.

The road ahead will bring new challenges. I am ready for them. My growth mindset is not a theory. It is a habit I live every day. And as long as I keep growing, so will everything I lead.

Embracing the Power of Reflection

One of the most underutilized tools in leadership is reflection. Many entrepreneurs rush from one task to the next, chasing deadlines and profits, never pausing to evaluate what is truly working. Reflection is more than looking back; it is the deliberate practice of analyzing, synthesizing, and internalizing lessons to propel yourself forward.

I schedule reflection intentionally. Once a week, I step away from operations and ask: What went right? What went wrong? What patterns am I noticing? Where did I react instead of lead? These moments often spark breakthroughs that daily busyness hides. Reflection also builds emotional intelligence. When I analyze interactions with clients, team members, or partners, I uncover not only business insights but personal ones: How did I respond under pressure? Did I communicate with clarity? Did I uphold my values even when challenged? These questions shape both my leadership and my character.

The Art of Strategic Patience

Entrepreneurship is often portrayed as fast-paced and relentless. While speed matters, patience is equally vital. Strategic patience is the ability to act with urgency when necessary but to wait when timing must align with long-term results.

I learned this early in luxury real estate. A high-value property may not sell immediately despite extensive marketing. Pushing too hard risks diminishing its perceived value. Instead, I focus on positioning, cultivating relationships with the right buyers, and creating anticipation. The results are consistently higher quality and more sustainable outcomes.

Patience also applies to team development. Leadership growth in others cannot be rushed. Mentoring, training, and providing space for independent decision-making take time. Impatience often leads to micromanagement, frustration, and erosion of morale. Strategic patience is a daily discipline I consciously practice.

The Compounding Effect of Small Wins

In business, it is easy to focus solely on the big wins the multimillion-dollar deal, the viral product launch, the high-profile client. But the foundation of lasting success is built on small, consistent wins. These wins compound over time, building credibility, confidence, and momentum.

I encourage emerging leaders to track these wins. Write them down. Reflect on them. They serve as proof that your daily actions are moving the needle, even when larger results are not yet visible. This habit builds resilience and reinforces the growth mindset I live by.

Resilience in the Face of Uncertainty

No entrepreneurial journey is immune to uncertainty. Markets fluctuate, consumer behavior shifts, and unexpected crises test even the strongest leaders. I have faced economic downturns, supply chain disruptions, and industry shifts that threatened to derail my progress. Each time, resilience determined the outcome.

Resilience is more than enduring challenges; it is proactive adaptability. It requires emotional stability, creativity, and the ability to make decisions under pressure. I cultivate resilience by focusing on what I can control: my actions, mindset, and preparation. I also ensure my team shares this resilience by modeling it consistently and creating systems that absorb shocks rather than break under them.

I remember a moment during a market downturn when a major client withdrew from a multimillion-dollar deal unexpectedly. Instead of panicking, I gathered my thoughts, analyzed options, and launched a creative marketing strategy. Within months we were back in discussions of other projects. Resilience is not passive it is a series of deliberate, confident actions in uncertainty.

Leveraging Influence, Not Authority

True leadership extends beyond authority. Influence is the currency of lasting impact. People follow leaders they respect, trust, and feel inspired by not those who command based solely on title.

I cultivate influence through authenticity, competence, and consistency. I communicate clearly, keep promises, and demonstrate expertise without arrogance. I empower my teams to contribute ideas and take ownership of outcomes. Influence emerges naturally from a culture where people feel seen, valued, and challenged to grow.

This principle has been particularly effective in mentoring women entrepreneurs. By focusing on influence rather than control, I inspire action, guide decision-making, and foster independence. The ripple effect extends beyond my direct impact, creating a new generation of confident, capable leaders.

Innovation Through Curiosity

Innovation is rarely a product of luck; it is the result of curiosity applied with discipline. Curiosity drives questions, exploration, and experimentation, but without focus, it becomes wasted energy.

I encourage my teams to explore ideas, test methods, and challenge assumptions. We treat failures as data, not disasters. This approach led to product lines in beauty that resonated with emerging consumer trends and innovative real estate investment strategies that leveraged market shifts before competitors noticed.

Curiosity also applies to personal growth. I read broadly across industries, attend conferences outside my core fields, and seek mentors from diverse backgrounds. This cross-pollination of ideas fuels innovative solutions that would not arise from a single perspective.

Balancing Risk and Prudence

Entrepreneurship requires risk, but indiscriminate risk is not leadership. I approach risk as calculated and informed. I evaluate potential impact, likelihood of success, and alignment with long-term goals. I take risks when opportunity outweighs uncertainty, but I never compromise foundational values for short-term gain.

An example from real estate illustrates this: a property in a less-traditional area had high upside potential but also higher risk. I conducted rigorous market analysis, consulted local experts, and developed contingency plans. The result: a successful investment that not only delivered profit but positioned my business ahead of market trends. Balancing risk with prudence ensures sustainable growth without reckless exposure.

The Emotional Intelligence Edge

Leadership is as much emotional as it is strategic. High emotional intelligence (EQ) distinguishes leaders who inspire loyalty from those who demand compliance. EQ allows you to read situations, understand motivations, and manage your own responses under stress.

I cultivate emotional intelligence by actively listening, observing team dynamics, and reflecting on my reactions. In client interactions, I anticipate concerns and respond proactively. In team management, I address conflict quickly, fairly, and with empathy. Emotional intelligence amplifies decision-making, strengthens relationships, and creates a culture that attracts talent and clients alike.

The Power of Strategic Networking

Networks are not simply collections of contacts; they are ecosystems of influence, knowledge, and opportunity. I approach networking with intentionality, ensuring each connection serves mutual value and aligns with my mission.

I invest time in building relationships with thought leaders, industry peers, mentors, and potential collaborators. These networks have been instrumental in scaling businesses, securing, and identifying emerging market trends. I focus on quality over quantity, nurturing connections with authenticity and strategic foresight.

Integrating Technology for Scalability

Modern leadership requires leveraging technology to scale effectively without sacrificing quality. I have embraced tools that enhance communication, data analysis, marketing automation, and customer engagement. Technology allows me to monitor performance, streamline operations, and free human energy for high-value decision-making.

However, technology is a tool, not a substitute for leadership. I maintain the human element in all operations, ensuring automation enhances rather than replaces personal connection. This balance has been crucial in maintaining brand loyalty while growing rapidly.

Financial Mastery as a Leadership Skill

Financial literacy is non-negotiable for leaders. Growth mindset and vision are insufficient without understanding cash flow, investment, and risk management. I prioritize financial mastery as a strategic tool, not a chore.

I track metrics meticulously, assess return on investment for initiatives, and plan for multiple contingencies. This discipline has allowed me to seize opportunities during downturns, make informed expansions, and secure the long-term viability of my ventures.

Creating a Culture of Excellence

Excellence is a habit, not a goal. I instill this philosophy throughout every organization I lead. Standards are clearly communicated, and accountability is expected. Excellence is reinforced through recognition, mentorship, and modeling the behaviors I value.

A culture of excellence attracts talent, retains clients, and differentiates a brand in saturated markets. It creates momentum where high performance becomes a shared expectation rather than an exception.

Storytelling as a Leadership Tool

I have learned that stories inspire action more effectively than facts alone. Sharing the narrative behind a product, project, or decision engages hearts as well as minds. Storytelling creates connection, clarifies purpose, and motivates people to align with a vision.

In my beauty business, I craft stories around each product, highlighting values, origins, and impact. In real estate, I narrate the vision behind properties, emphasizing community transformation, design philosophy, and long-term potential. This approach cultivates loyalty, trust, and emotional investment in my ventures.

Harnessing the Psychology of Motivation

Understanding what drives people is a powerful tool for leadership. Motivation is rarely uniform; it is personal, situational, and dynamic. I tailor my approach based on individual drivers recognition, challenge, autonomy, or impact.

By understanding these dynamics, I create environments where people perform not because they are forced to, but because they want to. Motivation combined with accountability yields sustainable high performance.

The Ripple Effect of Influence

Every decision, action, and interaction creates a ripple. I lead with the awareness that my influence extends beyond immediate results. How I collaborate, and communicate shapes perceptions, behaviors, and opportunities downstream.

By being deliberate in my actions, I maximize positive ripple effects creating networks of empowered individuals, and teams who elevate each other. The long-term impact of leadership is measured in these ripples.

The Courage to Pivot

Pivoting is not failure; it is informed adaptation. I have shifted strategies, product lines, and business models multiple times. Each pivot required courage to let go of the familiar, analyze new opportunities, and act decisively.

A successful pivot is grounded in vision and discipline. It does not abandon core principles; it aligns them with changing realities. Courage without preparation is reckless; discipline without courage is stagnant. Both are required.

Practical Takeaways for Readers

From my journey, I offer practical steps for those ready to elevate their leadership and business mindset:

1. Decide on your standards and keep them, even under pressure.
2. Build relationships before you need them.
3. Focus on the client's experience, not only the transaction.
4. Study your setbacks for patterns and lessons.
5. Create systems that protect your energy and time.
6. Adapt faster than your competitors without losing your values.
7. Invest in your own education every year.

Purpose-Driven Impact

Beyond profits, I built my work around impact. I mentor women in business, guiding them to think strategically about growth and sustainability. I believe entrepreneurship is a tool for freedom, but only if you build it with intention.

Collaborate with others like minded individuals, sharing tools and resources that will make an impact in both each other's businesses and lives. I remind them that growth without purpose is empty. Every decision should connect to a bigger mission.

Future Vision

I am building businesses that will outlast me. I see a future where my work inspires others to lead boldly, think forward, and expand what they believe is possible. My vision is global. I aim to connect with leaders, innovators, and dreamers who are ready to create value in their own communities.

My story is still being written. The challenges ahead will require the same growth mindset that brought me here. And I will continue to choose growth. Every day.

Natalie Horseman

Horseman Publishing

https://www.instagram.com/thefamilyremixguide/
nataliehorseman.comgoatonthegobooks.com

Natalie Horseman, MSN, RN, is a dedicated nurse with nearly two decades of experience in child and family development. Her extensive background in healthcare has equipped her with a profound understanding of resilience and strength. Throughout her career, Natalie has been committed to guiding individuals through life's most challenging moments with both compassion and empathy. Her personal journey of overcoming adversity has deeply fueled her passion for empowering others. Through her writing, Natalie combines practical advice with heartfelt encouragement, creating a sense of community for those navigating life's storms. She believes that while our experiences shape us, they do not define us. Through her contributions, Natalie strives to inspire readers to embrace their inner strength and resilience, offering reassurance that they are never alone on their journey.

The Self-Doubt Detox

By Natalie Horseman

The Poison We Drink Daily

Self-doubt is the poison we willingly drink, drop by drop, until it courses through our veins like a toxin we can't remember life without. It doesn't announce itself with warning labels or bitter tastes. Instead, it masquerades as wisdom, as caution, as the responsible voice that keeps us from making fools of ourselves. It whispers lies so consistently that they begin to sound like truth. You're not qualified. You're not ready. You're not enough. These words become the soundtrack to our lives, the invisible chains that keep us small, safe, and stuck.

But here's the insidious part: we don't just tolerate this poison; we defend it. We convince ourselves that self-doubt is humility, that questioning our abilities is wisdom, that staying small is noble. We mistake the prison for protection, the limitation for prudence.

For years, I carried self-doubt like a security blanket: uncomfortable but familiar. It lived in the space between my dreams and my actions, creating a chasm so wide that I convinced myself it was protection rather than prison. It told me it was keeping me humble, keeping me realistic, keeping me from the inevitable disappointment of reaching too high. It convinced me that the voice in my head questioning every decision was my intuition, when in reality, it was my fear.

I watched as self-doubt robbed me of opportunities I was qualified for, silenced me in meetings where my voice mattered, and kept me playing small in a world that desperately needed what I had to offer. I saw other people (sometimes less experienced, sometimes less prepared) step into roles I had dreamed of, while I remained on the sidelines, convinced I wasn't ready yet.

The truth I've come to understand after decades of this toxic relationship is this: Self-doubt isn't wisdom. It's fear dressed up as prudence. It's not protecting you from failure.

It's guaranteeing it.

I've spent decades swimming in the murky waters of self-doubt, drinking its poison daily, and I can tell you with absolute certainty—it's not serving you. It's not protecting you. It's not keeping you humble or realistic or safe. It's slowly suffocating the very essence of who you're meant to become, dimming the light that the world needs you to shine.

The woman who changes lives, who leads with conviction, who creates and innovates and inspires, isn't the one who waits until she feels ready. She's the one who acts despite the doubt, who moves forward carrying her fears rather than being paralyzed by them.

The antidote exists. The detox is possible. But first, you have to stop drinking the poison.

The Anatomy of Self-Doubt

Self-doubt doesn't announce itself with fanfare. It's subtle, insidious, weaving itself into the fabric of our thoughts until we can't tell where our authentic voice ends and the doubt begins. It speaks in familiar tones, sometimes sounding like a concerned parent, other times like a harsh critic, but always with the same underlying message: You are not capable of more.

For me, self-doubt showed up as the voice that questioned every decision before I made it. It was the pause before I raised my hand in meetings, the hesitation before I submitted my writing, the endless spiral of "what ifs" that kept me awake at night. It convinced me that everyone else had received some secret manual for life that I'd somehow missed, that success was reserved for people who were inherently different from me.

Self-doubt fed on my imposter syndrome like fuel to a fire. Every promotion, every achievement, every compliment was filtered through its lens: They'll figure out you don't belong here soon enough. It turned my accomplishments into evidence of luck rather than competence, my successes into flukes rather than results of my efforts.

But the most insidious part of self-doubt isn't how it questions our abilities. It's how it shapes our identity. Slowly, imperceptibly, we begin to see ourselves through its distorted lens. We become the person who "can't," who "shouldn't," who "isn't." We shrink to fit the small box that doubt has constructed for us.

The Shadows Self-Doubt Creates

Self-doubt didn't just whisper in my ear. It roared, drowning out any possibility of seeing myself clearly. It showed up everywhere, poisoning every aspect of how I moved through the world. I convinced myself I wasn't good enough or pretty enough to deserve a serious relationship. I believed people would judge my character based on how I looked, on the size of my body, reducing my worth to a number on a scale or a reflection in a mirror.

In professional settings, self-doubt whispered that I wasn't intelligent enough for certain opportunities, that my ideas weren't valuable enough to share. I learned to keep my thoughts and feelings locked away, convinced they were burdens others shouldn't have to carry. The woman who had so much to offer the world became a master at making herself invisible.

What started as self-doubt metastasized into something far more destructive: self-consciousness that analyzed every word I spoke, every move I made, followed by self-loathing that ate away at any sense of worth I might have had. I found myself in a dark hole that seemed to have no bottom, wanting nothing more than to cover myself up and hide from a world that felt too harsh, too judgmental, too ready to confirm my worst fears about myself.

I developed an all-or-nothing mentality that made healing impossible. No matter what small action I took for my mental or physical health (a walk around the block, a moment of self-care, a tiny step toward a goal), it was never enough. The voice in my head demanded perfection or declared everything worthless. There was no middle ground, no space for progress, no room for the messy, imperfect journey that real growth requires.

So, I retreated. I dove into my work, using professional achievement as both shield and sword: proof that I was valuable while simultaneously hiding the immense torture I was experiencing inside. I became skilled at compartmentalizing, at presenting a competent facade while internally drowning in self-criticism and shame.

Self-doubt doesn't just question our abilities—it hijacks our identity, convincing us that we are our limitations rather than the limitless beings learning to navigate them.

The Cost of Staying Small

The price of living in self-doubt's shadow isn't paid all at once. It's extracted slowly, opportunity by opportunity, decision by decision, until you look up one day and realize how much life you've left unlived.

I think about the promotion I never applied for because I convinced myself I needed "just one more year" of experience. By the time I felt ready, the position was filled by someone with half my qualifications but twice my confidence. I think about the ideas I never shared in strategy meetings, watching as someone else presented a similar concept weeks later to widespread acclaim. I think about the relationships I sabotaged because I couldn't believe someone could love me without an agenda.

The compound effect of these small hesitations became staggering. Each time I chose silence over speaking up, safety over risk, I was training my brain that I wasn't worth the space I occupied. I was teaching myself to be smaller, quieter, less visible. I was becoming a master of my own diminishment.

But perhaps the heaviest cost was the energy it took to constantly monitor myself. Self-doubt is exhausting. It requires enormous mental bandwidth to question every thought, second-guess every decision, and analyze every interaction for evidence of your inadequacy. I lived in a state of hypervigilance, constantly scanning for threats to my already fragile sense of self-worth.

The physical toll was undeniable, too. Chronic self-doubt manifested in tension headaches, sleepless nights, and a nervous energy that left me feeling drained even when I hadn't accomplished anything meaningful. My body was holding the stress of trying to be perfect while believing I was fundamentally flawed.

I watched other women step boldly into opportunities that terrified me. They weren't more qualified, more talented, or more deserving. They simply believed they had the right to try. While I was busy perfecting my credentials and waiting for permission, they were out there creating the lives I only dared to dream about.

The greatest tragedy isn't falling short of your potential. It's never discovering what that potential actually is because you were too afraid to test it.

The cost of staying small ripples outward, too. When we don't speak up, the people who need to hear our voices are left in silence. When we don't pursue our dreams, the problems we're uniquely equipped to solve remain unsolved. When we don't step into our power, we rob the world of our contributions and rob ourselves of the life we're meant to live.

The Choice to Find Myself

The journey out of that darkness wasn't quick or linear. It required something I had never given myself before: the conscious choice to believe I was worth the effort of healing. It took extensive self-reflection, therapy, and time to dig myself out of the hole I had fallen into. More than that, it required changing not just my actions, but my entire way of thinking about myself.

I had to learn to take small actions (tiny, imperfect steps) and then do something revolutionary: recognize and celebrate those steps as progress. Instead of dismissing a five-minute walk as "not real exercise," I learned to honor it as movement. Instead of berating myself for imperfect efforts, I began to see them as evidence of courage.

Learning to show myself grace became a daily practice. I had to face my past and trauma, not to wallow in it or use it as an excuse, but to understand how it had shaped my inner dialogue. Most importantly, I had to accept that my story doesn't define me. It's part of me, but it's not the whole of me.

The most profound shift came when I learned to be happy in the space I was in, rather than constantly measuring myself against some impossible standard of where I thought I should be. This didn't mean settling or giving up on growth—it meant finding peace in the present moment while still moving forward.

Healing isn't about erasing your story—
it's about rewriting your relationship with it.

You are not broken; you are becoming.

That choice (to own my story, to claim my worth, to step out of the shadows) changed everything. Not because it eliminated self-doubt forever, but because it gave me the tools to recognize it as the unreliable narrator it had always been.

The Ripple Effect

As I began to trust myself more, something beautiful happened—the people around me began to see me differently, too. When I stopped apologizing for my ideas, others started taking them more seriously. When I stopped qualifying my expertise, others began to see me as the expert I had always been.

My team at work noticed the change immediately. Instead of the hesitant leader who second-guessed every decision, they saw someone who could make tough calls with conviction. My confidence gave them permission to trust my judgment, which in turn reinforced my growing belief in myself. Team meetings transformed from cautious discussions where I hedged every suggestion with "maybe" and "I could be wrong, but..." to dynamic sessions where I could present ideas with clarity and conviction.

The shift in my personal relationships was equally profound. I stopped attracting people who confirmed my worst fears about myself and began drawing in those who saw my value clearly. Friends who had grown accustomed to my self-deprecating jokes and constant apologies were surprised and delighted to see me speak about my accomplishments without immediately undermining them.

I learned to receive compliments without the reflexive "Are you sure?" or "I just got lucky" or "You're just being nice." When someone praised my work, I started responding with a simple "Thank you": two words that felt revolutionary after years of deflection. I began to accept help without feeling like a burden, to ask for what I needed without apologizing for having needs.

When we stop shrinking ourselves to fit other people's comfort zones, we give them permission to grow beyond theirs, too.

Perhaps most surprisingly, my newfound confidence created space for others to shine brighter, too. When I stopped competing for the title of "most humble person in the room," my colleagues felt free to share their own achievements. When I stopped downplaying my expertise, it gave others permission to claim theirs.

The children's book I had dreamed of writing for twenty years finally made it from idea to reality because I stopped waiting for permission I didn't need. The anthology chapters I contributed came from a place of knowing I had something valuable to share, rather than hoping someone might find me worthy of inclusion.

Opportunities began appearing that I never would have noticed before (speaking engagements, collaboration requests, leadership roles), not because they hadn't been there, but because I was finally ready to see myself as someone worthy of such invitations. The world hadn't changed; my willingness to participate in it had.

The Practical Detox: Five Essential Strategies

Through my journey, I've developed five core strategies that form the foundation of an effective self-doubt detox. These aren't one-time fixes but daily practices that build resilience against doubt's persistent whispers.

1. The Reality Check Protocol

When self-doubt strikes, I've learned to treat it like a fact-checking exercise. I ask myself three questions:

- What evidence supports this doubt?
- What evidence contradicts it?
- What would I tell a friend facing this same doubt?

This process takes doubt out of the emotional realm and into the logical one, where it can be examined objectively rather than felt overwhelmingly.

Real-world example: When doubt whispered, "You're not qualified to lead this project," I would write down:

- *Evidence supporting:* "I've never led a project this large before."

- *Evidence contradicting:* "I successfully managed three smaller projects, my supervisor specifically chose me for this role, and I have the technical skills required."
- *What I'd tell a friend:* "You were selected for this position because someone believes in your abilities. Trust their judgment and your own track record."

Practice this: The next time you catch yourself in a spiral of self-doubt, pause and write down your answers to these three questions. Notice how often the evidence against your doubt outweighs the evidence supporting it.

2. The Competence Collection

I maintain an ongoing collection of evidence of my competence, not to feed my ego, but to balance the scales that doubt tips toward inadequacy. This includes:

- Screenshots of positive feedback
- Lists of accomplishments, both big and small
- Photos from moments when I felt proud and confident
- Notes about challenges I've overcome

Sample entries from my collection:

- Email from a colleague: "Your presentation changed how I think about this issue entirely."
- Personal note: "Successfully advocated for my salary increase, asked for what I was worth and got it."
- Photo: Me receiving my nursing leadership certification, beaming with pride.
- Challenge overcome: "Navigated the budget crisis by finding creative solutions that saved the department $50K."

Practice this: Start your own competence collection this week. Include anything that reminds you of your capabilities, growth, and resilience. Refer to it whenever doubt tries to convince you that you're not enough.

3. The Action Despite Doubt Approach

Instead of waiting for doubt to disappear before taking action, I've learned to act alongside it. This means applying for opportunities I don't feel "ready" for, sharing ideas before they feel "perfect," and saying yes to invitations that scare me.

How this looks in practice:

- Submitting the proposal even though my inner critic is screaming about typos I might have missed
- Raising my hand in the meeting while my heart pounds with the fear of saying something stupid
- Accepting the speaking invitation while simultaneously planning what I'll do if I forget my words

The key is acknowledging the doubt without letting it drive the decision. I might think, "I'm terrified I'll mess this up, AND I'm going to do it anyway because the potential for growth outweighs the risk of imperfection."

Practice this: Identify one action you've been avoiding due to self-doubt. Take one small step toward it this week, carrying the doubt with you rather than waiting for it to leave.

4. The Inner Critic Dialogue

I've learned to have conversations with my self-doubt rather than being consumed by it. I acknowledge its presence but challenge its authority.

Sample dialogue: *Inner Critic:* "You're not qualified enough for this leadership role." *Me:* "I hear that you're worried I'm not qualified enough, but I'm going to move forward anyway because the evidence shows I am prepared for this challenge. You're trying to protect me from failure, but staying small guarantees the very failure you're trying to prevent."

Inner Critic: "Everyone will see that you don't belong here." *Me:* "Thank you for trying to keep me safe, but I was invited here because someone saw value in what I bring. I'm going to trust their judgment and focus on contributing rather than hiding."

Practice this: The next time self-doubt arises, try speaking to it directly. Thank it for trying to protect you, then explain why you're choosing to move forward despite its concerns.

5. The Support System Activation

One of doubt's favorite tactics is isolation: convincing us that we're the only ones who struggle with these feelings. Building and activating a support system that can offer perspective when doubt clouds our vision is essential.

My support system includes:

- A mentor who reminds me of my growth when I can't see it
- A close friend who calls out my self-sabotaging language
- A colleague who celebrates my wins when I dismiss them as luck
- A therapist who helps me recognize patterns and develop new responses

How I activate this system: Instead of suffering in silence, I reach out: "I'm having one of those days where I feel like I don't know what I'm doing. Can you remind me of some evidence that contradicts this feeling?"

Practice this: Identify three people in your life who see your capabilities clearly. Share your doubts with them and ask for their honest perspective. Often, others can see our strengths more clearly than we can.

The Self-Doubt Detox Emergency Kit

Sometimes self-doubt hits like a sudden storm: intense, overwhelming, and demanding immediate attention. For these moments, you need quick, accessible tools that can interrupt the spiral before it gains momentum.

The 5-Minute Techniques for Acute Doubt Episodes

The 5-4-3-2-1 Grounding Method: When doubt creates anxiety, ground yourself in the present moment:

- 5 things you can see
- 4 things you can touch
- 3 things you can hear
- 2 things you can smell
- 1 thing you can taste

This pulls you out of the future-focused fears that doubt creates and anchors you in reality.

The Evidence Hunt: Set a timer for 3 minutes and list every piece of evidence you can think of that contradicts your current doubt. Write quickly, without editing. Include everything from major accomplishments to small acts of competence.

The Friend Test: Ask yourself: "If my best friend came to me with this exact doubt, what would I tell them?" Then give yourself the same compassionate, rational advice you'd offer someone you love.

Power Phrases That Actually Work

Unlike generic affirmations, these phrases are designed to acknowledge doubt while choosing action:

- "I can feel doubt and still move forward."
- "This feeling doesn't define my capability."

- "Courage isn't the absence of fear. It's action in the presence of it."
- "I don't need to feel ready to be ready."
- "My worth isn't determined by my comfort level."

Physical Reset Techniques

Power Posture: Stand tall, shoulders back, hands on hips (yes, like a superhero) for 2 minutes. Research shows this actually changes your hormone levels and increases confidence.

Breathing Reset: Inhale for 4 counts, hold for 4, exhale for 6. This activates your parasympathetic nervous system and reduces anxiety.

Movement Break: Do 10 jumping jacks, take a brisk walk around the block, or dance to one song. Physical movement interrupts the mental loop of doubt.

Emergency Contacts and Resources

Keep a list easily accessible of:

- Three people you can text when doubt strikes
- Your therapist's contact information
- One book or podcast that always helps you feel empowered
- Your competence collection (digital file or physical folder)

Common Detox Challenges and How to Navigate Them

The journey out of self-doubt isn't a straight line, and certain challenges appear so consistently that they deserve their own roadmap.

When Family and Friends Resist Your Growth

As you begin to step into your power, some people in your life may feel uncomfortable with the change. They might make comments like "You're getting too big for your britches" or "Remember where you came from." This resistance often stems from their own discomfort with staying small.

How to navigate this:

- Remember that their discomfort is about them, not you
- Set gentle but firm boundaries: "I appreciate your concern, but I'm choosing to pursue this opportunity"
- Find new communities that celebrate growth rather than discourage it
- Don't dim your light to make others comfortable

Handling the Guilt of Taking Up Space

Many of us, especially women, have been conditioned to believe that taking up space is selfish. As you begin to speak up, pursue opportunities, and claim your worth, guilt may arise.

Reframe the guilt:

- Taking up space isn't selfish. It's necessary for the contribution you're meant to make
- By modeling confidence, you give others permission to do the same
- The world needs your voice, your ideas, and your unique perspective
- Staying small serves no one

Dealing with Setbacks Without Giving Up

You'll have days when the old doubt returns with a vengeance. You might make a mistake, face rejection, or simply feel overwhelmed. These setbacks don't mean you're back to square one.

Setback recovery strategy:

- Acknowledge the feeling without judgment: "I notice I'm feeling doubtful again"
- Remember that healing isn't linear. Setbacks are part of the process
- Use your emergency kit tools
- Reach out to your support system
- Focus on the next small step, not the entire journey

Managing the Discomfort of Being Seen

Stepping out of self-doubt's shadow means accepting visibility, which can feel terrifying after years of hiding. You might feel exposed, vulnerable, or like you're wearing a spotlight.

Comfort strategies for visibility:

- Start small. Share one idea in a meeting before giving a presentation
- Remember that most people are focused on themselves, not scrutinizing you
- Practice receiving attention positively. Let compliments land instead of deflecting them
- Celebrate the courage it takes to be seen

The Ongoing Journey

I wish I could tell you that completing a self-doubt detox means never experiencing doubt again, but that would be a lie. Doubt still visits me, sometimes as a whisper, sometimes as a roar. The difference is that I no longer mistake its voice for truth or let it dictate my choices.

Some days, I feel powerful and confident, ready to take on any challenge. Other days, the old familiar doubts creep in, questioning my worth, my abilities, my right to take up space. But now I have the tools to navigate these moments without being derailed by them.

I've learned that self-doubt is often a sign that I'm growing, that I'm pushing against the edges of my comfort zone. Instead of seeing it as evidence that I should retreat, I now recognize it as confirmation that I'm moving forward. Growth doesn't come without resistance. Self-doubt is often just fear dressed up as caution, showing up when I'm on the brink of becoming more.

***Growth and doubt often travel together.
The question isn't whether you'll feel doubt, but whether you'll let it drive your decisions.***

The goal isn't to eliminate doubt entirely. It's to change your relationship with it. To see it as one voice among many, rather than the authoritative narrator of your story. To acknowledge its presence without giving it power over your choices.

Your Detox Invitation

If you've recognized yourself in these pages, if the poison of self-doubt has been coursing through your veins for too long, I want you to know that detox is possible. It's not easy, and it's not quick, but it's absolutely achievable.

You don't have to wait until you feel ready. You don't have to wait until the doubt disappears. You can begin right now, right where you are, with whatever small step feels possible.

Your detox might look like:

- Applying for that position you've been watching from afar
- Sharing your ideas in the next meeting instead of keeping them to yourself
- Starting the project you've been "preparing" for indefinitely

- Saying yes to the opportunity that both excites and terrifies you
- Speaking up for yourself when you typically stay silent
- Setting a boundary you've been afraid to establish
- Pursuing the dream you've been dismissing as unrealistic

Remember, courage isn't the absence of doubt. It's the decision to act in spite of it. Every time you choose action over hesitation, growth over safety, truth over the lies doubt tells, you're building immunity against its poison.

The Antidote Is Action

The most powerful antidote to self-doubt isn't confidence. It's action. Each time we act despite our doubts, we prove to ourselves that we're capable of more than our fears suggest. We build evidence that contradicts doubt's narrative and create new neural pathways that support self-trust instead of self-sabotage.

Your dreams are not too big. Your goals are not unrealistic. Your voice is not unworthy of being heard. The only thing standing between you and the life you're meant to live is the decision to stop letting doubt drive your choices.

Action creates evidence, evidence builds confidence, and confidence fuels more action. It's a beautiful cycle that begins with a single brave step forward.

You are not your doubts.

You are the person who has survived every challenge life has thrown at you.

You are the person who has grown stronger with each setback.

You are the person who has everything within you to create the life you envision.

Rising Beyond Doubt

As you begin your own self-doubt detox, remember that this isn't a journey you have to take alone. Every person who has ever achieved something meaningful has walked this path, has wrestled with these same whispers of inadequacy, has had to choose courage over comfort.

Your doubt doesn't make you weak. It makes you human. Your struggles don't disqualify you from success. They prepare you for it. Your fears don't define your limits. Your actions do.

The world needs what you have to offer. Not the perfect, polished version you think you need to become, but the real, imperfect, beautifully human you that exists right now. Your perspective, your ideas, your unique way of seeing and solving problems—these are gifts that only you can give.

Stop waiting for permission. Stop waiting for certainty. Stop waiting for the doubt to disappear.

Start now. Start scared. Start imperfect. But start.

Your life is waiting on the other side of your self-doubt. And I promise you: The woman you become when you stop listening to doubt's lies is more magnificent than you can currently imagine.

The detox begins with a single decision: to stop drinking the poison of self-doubt and start nourishing yourself with the truth of your worth.

You are ready. You are enough. You have always been enough.

Now go prove it to yourself.

Dr. Jasmine Zinck

Founder of Focused Victory LLC

https://www.linkedin.com/in/jasmine-zinck
https://www.facebook.com/Jasmine.Zinck8/
https://instagram.com/dr.jasminezinck
https://focusedvictory.com
https://seekyourfocusedvictory.com

As a Doctor of Philosophy specializing in Spiritual Healing and an Ordained Metaphysical Minister, I am dedicated to guiding individuals on their spiritual journeys toward mental, emotional, and spiritual well-being. As a Severe Traumatic Brain Injury survivor, I experienced a profound illumination and miraculous healing, which deepened my understanding of divine restoration and ignited my passion to help others find their own transformation. My practice blends scientific principles with spiritual wisdom, offering a holistic approach to healing that embraces both the seen and unseen dimensions of wellness. In service to God, I teach the Way to Spiritual Awakening and Victory, empowering individuals to reconnect with their innate divine essence. Through my work, I inspire others to embrace their own healing journey, unlocking their potential for wholeness, clarity, and spiritual rejuvination.

It's About Time: Your True Spirit Is Willing

By Dr. Jasmine Zinck

Awaken the Healer Within: Aligning Your Mindset with Focused Affirmations, Meditation, and Mystical Oneness

There was a time in my life when I believed my suffering was mine alone to carry—an unseen wound tucked beneath the surface of resilience. But as I peeled back the layers of my story, I began to see that I was not alone. In fact, I was part of a staggering collective: women who, like me, had survived both the terror of partnership abuse and the lingering shadows of traumatic brain injury.

My turning point came long before I ever knew the names University of Metaphysics or University of Sedona. In 2008, during one of the most harrowing chapters of my life, I suffered a traumatic brain injury so severe that many would have expected lasting impairment. But what came next could only be described as miraculous. Amid the confusion and pain, I was enveloped by the healing presence of Jesus Christ. It wasn't gradual. It wasn't ordinary. It was beyond extrasensory perception. It was God-driven supernatural—an unexplainable restoration that not only mended my brain but opened the doorway to my spiritual enlightenment.

Years later, in 2020, I came across a CDC report that shattered me and confirmed me all at once. One in every four women in the United States had experienced brain trauma during partner abuse. Even more sobering—one in nine people in America has survived a traumatic brain injury from abuse. That was when my inner knowing thundered to the surface: This is a part of my True Identity. Not just to thrive, but to understand, to awaken, and to guide others. For my spirit is willing! (Matthew 26:41).

Without formal enrollment, my doctoral research in philosophy with a focus on Spiritual Healing had already begun. It started with asking hard questions and trusting downloads via the Holy Spirit. I knew then that God's grace had not simply carried me through—it had positioned me for purpose. I was called not only to study healing but to become a facilitator for God. To bridge the chasm between neuroscience and soul consciousness. We are sculpted in the image of the Eternal One, endowed with an inner intelligence that remembers wholeness. Healing isn't just something we hope for— it's a sacred function of our design.

I now stand as a living proof that profound restoration is real. That we are not just brains and bodies, but energy, consciousness, and divinity wrapped in infinite light. And that with love, alignment, and holy surrender, the soul itself can rise—whole and radiant—from the ashes of any trauma, while tuned into the Perfect Mind of the Universe and God.

With each isolated incident of traumatic brain injury, the clinical numbers and diagnostic statistics paint only part of a much larger, poignant picture. Every year, millions of individuals suffer from TBIs—a collective testament to the sudden, external forces that can alter lives in an instant. These injuries, often induced not only by falls, accidents, or sports mishaps but also by the less-discussed concussive impacts, frequently manifest as complex syndromes. From the onset, many survivors grapple with conditions such as ADD, OCD, ADHD, anxiety, fatigue, mental blocks, mood swings, high irritability, bouts of anger, low self-esteem in social interactions, depression, and even multiple-personality disorders. The underlying thread connecting these diverse psychological and neurobiological disturbances is often an unseen, unresolved brain injury. Without diagnosis or proper treatment, people often turn to unhealthy coping mechanisms, unintentionally compounding the very pain they're trying to escape. "Understanding the functions and problems of [the parts of] the brain is often essential to the healing process of people who suffer" (Daniel Amen, 2000).

In 2024, as I embarked upon the journey of formulating my dissertation, I was driven by a fervent desire to challenge conventional medical narratives. My thesis was bold, yet divinely inspired: that through the conscious harnessing of Prana—the very essence of our Life Force—we can transcend traumatic brain injuries, reconnect with our inherent I Am Presence, and ultimately experience full, profound recovery. This work was not merely academic; it was a spiritual calling. I have since proven that the Infinite Universal Energy Source, which I believe is the very manifestation of God's Holy Spirit Power, heals those whose lives have been truncated by TBIs. What is most astonishing is that God, in His infinite grace, revealed to me that many neurobiological disorders are misdiagnosed. Conditions such as attention deficits, obsessive tendencies, and even mood dysregulation may actually be rooted in unresolved traumatic brain injuries. "Post-traumatic OCD has a relatively specific pattern of symptoms even in patients with mild TBI and is associated with a variety of other psychiatric disorders" (Marcos Grados, 2003).

Traumatic brain injury, by its very nature, occurs when a sudden, external physical force disrupts the delicate equilibrium of the brain, often setting off a cascade of long-lasting neurological and psychological challenges. The journey of recovery is fraught with obstacles, as symptoms—whether stemming from minor concussions or severe injuries—can emerge months or even years after the initial trauma. Yet, this chapter is about mind transformation. It is an invitation to "dissolve, great physical pain and emotional loss when you stop looking at it and for it" (Penney Pierce, 2011). We can begin to heal both physically and spiritually, using Metaphysical Science principles and practices of spiritual mind treatments. This is more than a scientific inquiry; it is a passionate declaration that every individual is entitled to a full and rewarding life—a birthright that can be reclaimed through the marriage of Christ Consciousness and transformative healing energy available to you in God's Presence.

When the microcosm of your mind and body is healed, the macrocosm follows suit. The process of healing begins and ultimately culminates with the Infinite Universal Energy Source, from which all creation flows and in which every soul finds its sanctuary. Life is meant to be a journey of spiritual growth. God, in His infinite wisdom, gave each of us life intentionally—a life designed to be lived with healthy intent and a positive purpose.

The first step toward becoming aware of your divine essence— whether you have been diagnosed with a neurobiological disorder known to stem from a traumatic brain injury (or one that remains undiagnosed)—is to cleanse your subconscious mind of negative thought energies. This negativity, which I have come to refer to as the Standard American Mindset, has seeped into the collective consciousness, fueled by the negative influence of television, limited views of news broadcasts, sitcoms, cable shows, online content, and even radio podcasts. To pave the way for true transformation, I recommend a period of fasting—not from healthy food, but from any form of distraction that veils your inner godlike nature. By temporarily canceling memberships and disconnecting from disruptive media, you set the stage for a cleansing process that allows the divine attributes of the Universal Mind, the Spirit within you, God, to shine forth with clarity and power.

A cleansed mind, brimming with pure and uplifting thoughts, becomes both the wellspring of inner happiness and the catalyst for positive outward expression. This undertaking requires the deliberate release of all negativity stored in the recesses of memory. Affirmations serve as potent tools to maintain a positive conscious mindset, yet true transformation requires that these affirmations transcend their surface level. By engaging in Focused Affirmations within a Light State of Meditation, you initiate the process of dissolving entrenched, outdated thought patterns. This space of inner stillness encourages the growth of new neural connections and reinforces the neural pathways toward expansion, resilience, love, and boundless possibility.

The fact is, 90% of our conscious thought is governed by our subconscious mind—the vast memory bank of our experiences, so the practice of Focused Affirmations is essential. Whether your affirmations are life-improving, goal-oriented, or simply aimed at alignment, they work to reprogram your internal dialogue. As you consciously affirm, cleansing your mind by releasing all past negative thought energy is essential in obtaining a transformed mind—a God-filled state of consciousness, replete with peace, love, and happiness—you fortify the connection between your outer life and the divine energy that resides within.

This transformative journey is beautifully underscored by scripture. Philippians 2:5-13 reminds us:

- "Let this mind be in you, which was also in Christ Jesus: For God is working in you, giving you the desire and the power to do what pleases him."

This passage reassures us that transformation is not solely our own doing—it is an active collaboration with the divine, as the Infinite Universal Mind, God, continuously guides and empowers us.

At its core, Prana—our Life Force—is pure energy. Energy is malleable; it transforms at will, cannot be created or destroyed, and is constant (Clara Moskowitz, 2014). Dr. Fritz Frederick Smith, MD, in *The Alchemy of Touch*, beautifully articulates that the vibratory nature of our energy can be harnessed as a healing tool. Energy, described in *The Revealing Word* by Charles Fillmore, is the inherent power of the Mind of God, the very essence that drives our thought and expression. This understanding aligns with the biblical promise found in Isaiah 40:28-31:

- "The Lord never grows weak or weary. He gives power to the weak and strength to the powerless. Those who trust in the Lord will find new strength. They will soar high on wings like eagles. They will run and not grow weary. They will walk and not faint."

Meditation has been proven by Neuroscience, Neuropsychiatry, Neuroplasticity, Western and Eastern medicine, Spiritual Healers, and Metaphysicians to have a powerful effect on healing the brain and body. Research confirms that regular meditation enhances attention, concentration, memory, and cognitive skills. As many people healing from a TBI have found, focusing on a singular object, idea, or activity during meditation acts as a powerful lens, directing the mind toward growth and clarity (Alice G. Walton, 2015).

"But seek ye first the Kingdom of God [within you] and his righteousness; and all these things will be added unto you" (Matthew 6:33).

"Chai" (חי) means life in Hebrew—a symbol of vitality.

During the three days I was left alone after the attack, all I could think about was life… and healing. I had once been a professional, licensed massage therapist, specializing in medical and sports massage. I understood energy—its different forms, its unseen rhythms. And I recognized that God is the Creator of All.

At some point, I realized it had been almost 24 hours since I'd last gone to the bathroom. I had no strength in my legs. I was dragging myself using my lower arms, unable to focus on standing, completely unaware of the full impact of my head injury. On the very first day, I went scent-blind. For six months, all I could smell was an intoxicating smoke. A psychiatrist friend later explained that it was likely damage to the nerves on my cribriform plate—burned from the trauma.

I curled up in a fetal position, facing the back of my oversized brown leather chair in the living room. Slowly, I began to rock from side to side. That gentle movement brought the slightest moment of relief—milliseconds, but enough. By holding onto those tiny fragments of ease, I found myself able to start forming conscious thoughts again.

I focused on what wasn't painful. And I began talking to God.

I thanked Him for my past, especially for the hands-on healing I'd once been able to give others through massage. I recalled how, before becoming a bartender, I had taken time off to heal from two simultaneous wrist fractures. That career detour had brought me to this dark place in the story. But I chose not to dwell on the pain or regret.

Instead, I remembered my purpose: healing and vitality.

I told God, "There is no reason I cannot be healed." I knew I was a Healer. I knew He was with me. There was no doubt in my heart that I could be made whole again.

And before my ego, my limited identity, could rise up and overanalyze, I was swept into the most breathtaking current—waves of black on black. The most beautiful I had ever seen.

In the Living Word (Bible KJV), the psalmist writes about these events. For more clarity, here are scriptures from Psalm 18:

[1] "I will love thee, O LORD, my strength. [2] The LORD is my rock, and my fortress, and my deliverer; My God, my strength, in whom I will trust; My buckler, and the horn of my salvation, and my high tower. [3] I will call upon the LORD, who is worthy to be praised: So shall I be saved from mine enemies. [4] The sorrows of death compassed me, And the floods of ungodly men made me afraid. [5]

The sorrows of hell compassed me about: The snares of death prevented me. [6] In my distress I called upon the LORD, And cried unto my God: He heard my voice out of his temple, And my cry came before him, even into his ears. [11] He made darkness his secret place; his pavilion round about him Were dark waters and thick clouds of the skies. [28] For thou wilt light my candle: The LORD my God will enlighten my darkness."

And so, He did.

There I was, floating on my back in still, black waters—completely at ease, free of the excruciating pain, and flooded with gratitude. I smiled and thought, "Thank you, God. I'm so glad You put me here instead of Heaven. I think the bright light and all the noise would've overwhelmed me."

Just then, a light began walking toward me—radiant and smiling. It was King Jesus. Smiling, He reached out His hand and asked gently, "Are you ready?" And I realized in that moment: I could see Him, but I couldn't see myself at all. I thought, he wore his hair long today!

My soul knew him, my personal ego mind or falsehood spirit in this world did not. I extended my right hand, shook His, and said with a laugh, "It's about time!"

Instantly, I was back in the chair, curled in a fetal position. My eyes shot open. I turned my head and could somehow see through the solid front door. It was the middle of the day—the sun glowing on the grass confirmed it. Then I heard a Voice: "Don't worry, someone is on their way."

I remember thinking, "I don't think I could even crawl to the car, much less drive safely." But I felt no panic. Just peace. Not even a headache. The pain didn't return until I arrived at the hospital.

I had, indeed, been scheduled for surgery. But as soon as the date was set, I was released. The surgeon—25 years of experience behind him—looked at me, stunned, and said, "I honestly don't know what to do with you except send you home." Three areas of brain bleeding. A hematoma the size of a baseball. Severe bruising of the brain. A fractured skull. All healed. The only thing left were faint signs of bruising on the CT scans.

In the end, the final diagnosis? Dehydration, mild anorexia, and a need for a doctor's note to excuse missed time at work.

Psalm 18: [30] "As for God, his way is perfect: The word of the LORD is tried: He is a buckler to all those that trust in him. [32] It is God that girdeth me with strength, And maketh my way perfect.[35] Thou hast also given me the shield of thy salvation: And thy right hand hath holden me up, and thy gentleness hath made me great.[46] The LORD liveth; and blessed be my rock; And let the God of my salvation be exalted. [47] It is God that avengeth me, [48] He delivereth me from mine enemies: Yea, thou liftest me up above those that rise up against me: Thou hast delivered me from the violent man. [49] Therefore will I give thanks unto thee, O LORD, among the heathen, And sing praises unto thy name. [50] Great deliverance [rescued, recovered, redeemed] giveth he to his [daughter]; And sheweth mercy to his anointed,... for evermore."

I was blessed with a full physical recovery—but neurologically, the way the brain processes trauma is something else entirely. It changes how you feel, how you show up in the world, even how you chase the goals you once held dear. No one really talked about that side of it. I was given another chance at life, but without the tools to explain that I wasn't the same person. I remembered everything—my subconscious felt intact—but I often wondered... was I still the same soul?

Spiritually, I knew who I was. But in the external world, I couldn't relate. For more than 13 years, I felt disconnected—adrift between who I had been and who I was becoming.

Since September 11, 2019, I've been actively seeking God and the Kingdom within, learning from Jesus Christ. Through this journey, I discovered that metaphysical science explores the many levels of the Mind, the layers of consciousness, and even the fascia of the soul, often accessed through deep meditative states.

Mystic simply means to consciously seek God—in everything and everyone. Mystical union in meditation is a profound experience, an illumination. It is entering into God's Presence, where you are surrounded by divine light and begin to radiate it from within.

With each new advance of medical science, there will come an increasing awareness of what real (mystically aware) Spiritual Healing Practitioners have always known: The human body is an energy field.

- All internal organs are energy fields.
- All matter in the human body (cells, bones, fluids, etc., anything having mass or substance) is a vibrating field of energy.
- Treating the condition of the human body, therefore, actually affects the underlying energy factors that support the physical existence of the body and its various components.
- "When you change the inner energy level, you change or affect the outer physical body manifestation" (Dr. Paul Leon Masters, 2013).

Due to the chaotic energy that may need to be released, be aware of the consequences of failure to treat the negative conditions of the mind. Hindrance of spiritual and evolutionary growth often results from mental unrest, leading to blocked deeper meditational experiences and restraint of intuitive guidance. This can cause health disturbances like tension, anxiety, insomnia, and escapism, attracting more negative conditions and people. It also invokes the negative side of others, creating life confusion and emotional unrest.

Such hindrances keep one stuck in the past, preventing positive future progress, and may lead to self-destruction and false martyrdom (Jasmine Zinck, 2025). More information about this and healing specific neurobiological disorders is found in my workbook; visit SeekYourFocusedVictory.com for more info. Holistic Spiritual Healing does not take the place of a medical professional.

It's an honor to have traveled through these many stages of healing with God. But now, I want to shift the focus—not on my path, but on you! If any part of this resonates with your soul, I'd love to walk with you in discovering where to begin and what resources can support your journey.

Healing is not a miracle reserved for a few; it's the divine echo of our original blueprint. Made in the image of God (Genesis 1:27), we were born with an inner physician—a divine capacity to regenerate, restore, and rise again, achieving Focused Victory.

It's about time you have a Mindset Mastery starter toolkit with instructions so you can improve your health, your happiness, and the overall success in your life!

First, you want to eliminate the negativity that you have control over. Next, you will improve your thoughts, feelings, and emotions using Focused Affirmations. You can use affirmations anytime you need to nullify or dissolve negative thinking patterns, so it is helpful to write them on cards and have them on hand. You will find that you'll have more success using Focused Affirmations at least twice a day during Affirmative Meditation—a light state of meditation—or before and after deep meditation or prayer.

To gain a light state of meditation, take a few deep, deliberate breaths in, clearing the conscious mind of any worries, to-dos, or thoughts in particular, where you will be stilling or quieting the mind.

Here are some Focused Affirmations I wrote during my Theocentric Psychology doctorate exam. Read them out loud, and when one or a few of them resonate with you, then use them for at least a week. You will then read them out loud, whisper and then to yourself to deeply transform your subconscious mind. Affirmations can also make you aware of your Unlimited Spiritual True Self.

- "I tune my mind inward to the higher vibrations of the Eternal One, wanting for nothing."
- "God's Will is my purpose, and my purpose is God's Will."
- "I dethrone my ego mind, and all negative thoughts are held captive and dissolved by my Christ Mind/Consciousness."
- "I am a manifestation of the Oneness of the Universe."
- Intuitional – "I am guided by Higher Intuition and with knowing this endeavor is successful by God's guidance and grace, flowing through me."
- Releasing – "I give all negativity and distractions to you, Father God, for your will be done and I will follow through!"
- Sleeping Beauty - "I declare that during my sleep, the Infinite Beauty of the Kingdom of Light, Love, and Health radiates in through and around me, bringing the glow of God to my physical appearance, this night and every night."
- Organized Living - "Upon waking up each day, I seek the Kingdom of God, for acknowledging Oneness with the Spirit is necessary for my logical mind to stay focused and organized."
- "Harmony of organized life is a necessity, and my internal clock that is kept by the Eternal One lets me know what project is most important and when to move on for balance as I participate in daily living."
- "My energy is conserved because I am overflowing with living water from Source, and therefore I am able to concentrate with my logical mind, focusing on the improvement of financial

and material matters, sharing love everywhere I go, healing, rejuvinating and experiencing Spiritual fulfillment as my Higher Intuition is my creative guide."

- "I dethrone my personal ego and let God take over my mind, my thoughts, my actions for this moment of every moment of every day."

- "I let go of my impulses, anxiety, stresses, anger, fears, or whatever else is hindering me at this moment of life to proceed, and let God renew my mind, my heart, my thoughts, my environment, my social life, and guide me to whatever else I need to be detached from."

- "I let go of my pride and selfish ways and let God guide me to how I can better someone else's life."

- "I surrender the so-called odds against me to God's Presence, whose Love fills whatever emptiness there may be, therefore, attracting love back in all aspects of life."

- "I recognize and declare that God is the Strength in my life and God's Energy replaces my personal energy and gives greater concentration of energy to accomplish what needs to be accomplished."

- "God already knows what is best for me, be it love, health, material needs, and anything else, and I am guided by the Spirit of God, or God's Universal Mind, with Unlimited Peace, Wisdom, and Knowledge to achieve all this and more."

- "Daily, I practice meditation knowing that it activates God's Power in me as I attune to the Presence of God in my mental being."

Visualization Meditation is fantastic to do to visualize God's Presence of Light filling you and surrounding you with pure white glistening light, and feeling the love emitting from that divine energy. This type of meditation is also helpful to refocus and stay on meeting schedules with less stress. Again, you will get into a light state of meditation, but this time you will use your Focused Eye, or

Mind's Eye, or imagination.

Remain on Meeting Schedules:

- Visualization: "I squint in the future and envision not just my enjoyment of completion of this endeavor, but all the individuals that will find success in their life with God, by me following through!"
- Affirm and Declare:
    o "I give my spirit of control to God so my house responsibilities can be delegated to others, so I stay motivated and on time with my project."
    o "I capture the confidence of others by reflecting responsibility, and that I care about their time and have integrity with the ability to meet schedules."
    o "I draw on a reserve of Spiritual Power from the Presence of God at the nucleus of my mind to stay on point with my project and get necessities accomplished daily."
- End In Gratitude: "For this and more I am Thankful for, I let it be so, and so it is!"

Prayer Treatment

This is affirming your faith that what God has to bless you with, you have already been blessed:

"I call forth into the Divine Presence of the All-powerful God of the Universe at the nucleus of my mind.

"God's Light removes the psychic darkness, allowing me to see my life more clearly.

"Bless my mind, soul, and spirit with the beauties of God's Reality in the Illumined light of wisdom, in Spirit and in truth, for this day and eternity.

"For Your Love and Grace upon my life, I give thanks... and so it is!"

In the black-on-black current of surrender, I didn't find answers—I was surrounded by God's Presence. I felt Life. And in that timeless field of God's light, I realized... it was never about returning to who I was. It was about knowing who I already am.

I share this not as a final word, but as a living testimony. Your healing, your rejuvenation, your inner restoration—it's not only possible, it's sacred. The tools are here. The path is lit. The way is within the mind. And the spirit within you is already willing. You just have to commit to God.

One Within Christ Mind Eternal, to – "Seek Your Focused Victory: In Truth, With Love, For Health, Using The Power of God! "

Eternal Peace & Love,
Dr. Jasmine Zinck, PhD
Focused Victory LLC

Works Cited

Amen, Daniel G., *Change Your Brain Change Your Life. The Breakthrough Program for Conquering Anxiety, Depression, Obsessiveness, Anger, and Impulsiveness.* New York, NY: Three Rivers Press, 2000, p. 132. Print.

Fillmore, Charles. *The Revealing Word.* Mansfield Centre, CT: Martino Publishing, 2014. Print.

Grados, Marcos A. "Obsessive-compulsive disorder after traumatic brain injury." Pubmed.ncbi.nlm.nih.gov, n.d. Web. Nov. 15, 2003.

Holy Bible: King James Version. YouVersion. Web. 2023.

Masters, Paul Leon. *Theocentric Psychology Doctoral Degree Modules.* 5 vols. Sedona, AZ: University of Sedona Publishing, 2013. Print.

Moskowitz, Clara, "Fact or Fiction? Energy Can Neither Be Created Nor Destroyed." Scientificamerican.com, n.d. Web. Aug. 5, 2014.

Peirce, Penney, *Frequency*. New York, NY: First Atria Books/Beyond Words trade paperback ed., August 2011, p. 74. Print.

Smith, Fritz Fredrick. *The Alchemy of Touch*. Taos, NM: Complementary Medicine Press, 2005. Print.

Walton, Alice G. "7 Ways Meditation Can Actually Change The Brain." Forbes.com, n.d. Web. Feb. 9, 2015.

Zinck, Jasmine. *Seek Your Focused Victory: In Truth, With Love, For Health, Using The Power of God!* Eight Mile, AL: Focused Victory LLC, 2025, p. 131. Print.

Douglas Clarke

Founder and CEO of Razorwire Productions, Soulmate Productions Inc., and Douglas Clarke Media Technology Consulting

https://www.linkedin.com/in/douglasaclarke/
https://www.instagram.com/douglas.clarke.official/
https://soulmateofficial.com/

Douglas Clarke is the writer, director, and music composer behind Soulmate, a play that made history by debuting and extending Off-Broadway in New York City after its sold-out premiere in Los Angeles a mere 8 months after its conception. A lifelong tech innovator, Clarke recently found a second home in theater as a leading actor. Soulmate was his first foray into writing. A San Francisco Bay Area native based in Los Angeles, Clarke is a boundary-pushing innovator with over 25 years of experience in both tech and entertainment. As Founder of Razorwire Productions, he has led countless creative projects in multiple forms of media including music, podcast, and photography. In tech, Clarke has a history of breaking new ground via his inventive work with DTS, THX, and his cable network clients at NBC Universal. Known for consistent trail blazing, Clarke's work is defined by his ability to push creative and technological boundaries in novel ways.

Evolving Our Thoughts

By Douglas Clarke

In the beginning of August 2024, at 47 years of age, my heart and life felt so full. I had just returned from an absolutely incredible vacation in Italy with my beautiful girlfriend of seven years. We attended a very close friend's wedding in Sardinia and followed that with a romantic tour of Sicily and southern Italy. I returned to what I had cultivated to be my dream job over the previous 10 years, leading technical strategy for a global media technology company with exciting projects and prospects in progress.

It then all, suddenly, evaporated. My girlfriend left me, pointing to traits in me about which she had long been insecure. These were qualities I loved within myself but had been compromising for her and the relationship, knowing deep inside that doing so wasn't the path to lasting happiness. A week later, my company had a massive layoff, citing economic projections that were falling short and needing to create a balanced plan for shareholders. Not only I, but also my mentor and several extremely talented colleagues were affected.

Either of these events alone would have devastated me. However, both of them happening at once jolted me into a radical change in perspective. Though it may have partially been a survival mechanism, I'd like to think that this shift came from years of personal philosophies and practices; borne from a combination of some transformational work I'd undertaken during a similar quarter-life crisis in my mid-twenties, along with nine years of incredible and intensive psychological therapy I'd also given myself at that time. This journey is enhanced by deep observations and learnings that I have spent my adult life absorbing, with intention, about the human condition. I study why we do what we do, what works and what doesn't, and why.

It may be a cliché, but the only constant in life that we can count on is constant change, and unfortunately, most of those changes are not on our schedule and not in our control. When everything in life does start to shift, including the very ground we stand on, it's helpful to begin to inventory and exercise some of the few things that we can consciously influence, starting with what is inside of us, our own body and mind.

Notice the use of the word "influence," and not "control." As much as we would like to think we can control our own mindset, it's not easy. If it were, we could fully be whoever we wanted to be, in any situation. However, with this book, and this chapter, you will have some tools—concepts, methods, and examples—to put your mind in a place that will best support your own mental health, positive outlook, and overall happiness.

When my world shifted following my breakup and layoff, and everything felt completely out of my control, some insights emerged that put me on a new path, and I began to live out an unreal creative journey that had me create a new play with my own original music called *Soulmate*. *Soulmate* opened in January of 2025 in Los Angeles and extended into February. It then officially opened Off-Broadway in New York City in April of 2025, extending into June. In this chapter, I'd like to share some of those insights with you and how they worked for me during those few short months. As we proceed, I will also challenge you to forge a path to your own insights by thinking deeper.

The Evolution of Thought

There is a point in any thought process where the process feels complete as a judgement is made. It seems that there is a set of collectively acceptable judgements that we can settle on, for example, that something is our own or someone else's fault, or that we always have bad luck, or that this is just a pattern that is bound to repeat. While there may be some truth to each of those judgments and the reasoning behind them, they do not need to end the thought process. We can choose to think further and deeper. We can choose to keep asking why, and maybe leave the question unanswered at the end instead of concluding with a judgement. I am often very happy to say "I don't know," instead of feeling that every question requires an answer or opinion. This overall approach is what I call evolving our thoughts. It may take more time and lead us to very uncomfortable places, but I think it does offer us a path to greater learning, better outcomes, and a truer sense of happiness and fulfillment.

There were many times that my own self-doubt and fear of the unknown worked against me, from my own mind, to thwart my progress towards creating my play production. This is where I had to leverage my heart, body, and soul to ground me in the physical reality and space that I take up in the world, to give me the knowledge that physically, I will survive and everything will be okay, creating the physical foundation that enabled me to evolve my thoughts beyond those fears. I didn't ignore the fears, but instead fully acknowledged them and felt them for what they were. This evolved my interpretation of the fears. Instead of having them trigger a stopping point, I ultimately used them as a guide as to where I needed to go in order to best learn and grow. This allowed me to honor each fear as I did my best to work through them.

Before we travel further along the processes that created the mindset from which I successfully created my play, I'd like to propose and explore some more foundational concepts from which we can then build the elements of this mindset. Though I may present some of these concepts as if they are factual, they are only representations of how I see and understand the world, from my own perspective. We all have a different perspective, and this writing offers only a glimpse into my own. What is true for me may not be true for another, but in lending ourselves to others' perspectives, we may learn something significant that can expand our own perspective and truth.

Our modern world is a fabric of humanity.

Some of us live a self-sufficient life, away from society, in nature, truly in touch with the earth as their sole provider. I envy those who have chosen this path, or who were perhaps born into it. Thousands of centuries of evolution have conditioned our minds and bodies into this way of life. However, for most of us reading this book, I would wager that this does not represent our reality. For most of us participating in what we call modern society, we live with a dependency on each other to sustain us.

Every aspect of our modern world, including all of our needs—food, shelter, purpose, and love—is created in cooperation with or provided by other people. This creates an inextricable link between us and countless others; many that we are aware of; but when considering the degrees of connection that support all of those that support us, we realize there is an entire fabric of interconnected humanity of which each of us is a part.

There are many aspects of our nature, exhibited by our mental state, developed through evolution, survival, and our own capacity of understanding, that keep this truth obscured as we think about our everyday life. This is further supported by our culture, where individualism is so valued. As we step through more of these concepts, it's helpful to keep this undeniable truth in mind as it provides a good background context for the balance that we can strive to reach, to keep ourselves thriving along with those with whom we share our resources. We are not alone in the world, and we benefit the most from a healthy mindset when we also support health for the human systems that support us.

We are our own creation.

I completed college with a bachelor's degree at 20 years old and moved to Germany immediately after graduating, following my girlfriend at the time during her junior year of college abroad. Since the day that I left home and got on the plane to cross the Atlantic, I have survived entirely on my own. In the 28 years since that day, I have learned the most foundational lesson that only I am responsible for myself. With that responsibility, however, comes the power of creation.

We sometimes feel that the world around us casts us in a role that we cannot escape from, or that others define us. It is true that others may perceive us in a certain way, just as we have a perception of others ourselves. The perception that a person holds, however, reflects the person more than it represents us, as we all truly know very little about others and draw from our own limited knowledge and experience to fill in the gaps. In that sense, their perception has little to do with us and certainly holds very little power or relevance to who we are and how we choose to present ourselves in the world.

Furthermore, taking responsibility for our own individual identities alone gives us the greatest power that we have to influence the perception that others carry. The ability to do so is not easy, however, and comes from practicing self-awareness with humility. With this awareness, we can build a better relationship with our own perspective, our own complete perception of reality, both within us and outside of us.

There is no objective reality.

At least not one that we, as human beings, have the collective ability to be aware of. Our consciousness, the nature of which is debated over countless philosophies, can only create a perspective. Contributions to this perspective include observation, fed by our own senses, as well as the thoughts and experiences that we continuously build throughout our lives in order to make sense of it all. There, of course, may also be more mysterious inputs, ingrained in our genes or influenced by external forces that we don't understand. However, no matter the process of formation, each of our own individual perspectives remains completely unique to each and every one of us alone. Though we would like to think that there is one common truth, one shared and objective reality, we unconsciously fabricate it.

Understanding and ruminating on this fundamental truth is extremely powerful. It allows us to be better responsible for our own reality and how it interacts with others'. When we don't assume that we have a shared understanding of reality as a default, we can better avoid unintentionally imposing our perspective onto others. Instead, we can bring an epistemic humility to our interactions that leads to a more effective understanding of and communication with others.

Humility may be the greatest single asset we have towards our own expansion.

I see many human attributes as a spectrum, where two diametrically opposite qualities share the same common space. One of those spectrums from which a human perspective may spring at any given time is from a blend of ego-driven thoughts and thoughts based in humility. I think that any human perspective will absolutely contain both, hence the spectrum, but I find that thoughts more "naturally" or *easily* fall into the ego-driven category.

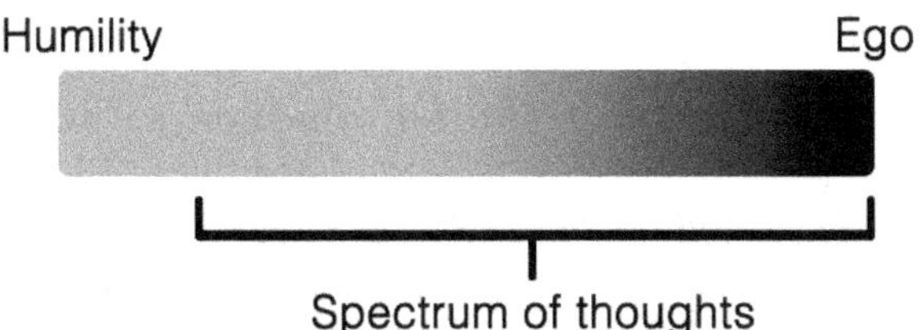

It sometimes takes deeper thought, which takes more time, with a degree of self-awareness to overcome the ego and therefore transform a thought into one more based in humility. In this context, ego represents a natural bias towards one's self; what one knows to be true, and what may favor one's self over others. While it may seem sensible to think and feel from this place, as it may not only feel comfortable, but *good*, as it may feed our own sense of worth, it becomes extremely limiting. However, we cannot completely expel the ego even if that was our sole focus. The nature of our own perspective means that, in a way, we can only work in our own self-interest, always doing the best that we can with what we know at the time. The evolution of our thoughts, in this case, is to adopt and therefore truly believe in the idea that acting with humility is boundless, and ultimately the best way for us to create and achieve what we want most in life in the fuller context of the fabric of humanity in which we co-exist. For me, these objectives are growth, expansion, connection, and happiness.

Building our integrity.

Integrity is pervasive as a concept. Just as we can visualize a building or structure with good integrity's being able to function optimally, having a lasting presence, and having the ability to persevere through extensive external and internal adversity, so can we visualize our own integrity. However, whereas we can build a structure once and have it be complete, the integrity that we build within ourselves is an unending intention and practice. I find it convenient that we can apply integrity to not only our physical bodies, but to our character, because I believe that both are extremely important, and contribute to our own strong base from which the application of each of these other concepts can be rooted.

Physical health, especially as we get older, is, by definition, foundational. If one is unable to maintain the balanced discipline of physical health, mainly through diet, exercise, and sleep, then it becomes exponentially more difficult to overcome other challenges downstream. Physical health is the basis of mental health. Our brain is housed by our bodies; the blood that circulates to our brain is pumped by our hearts, the nutrition that feeds our brain tissue is consumed by us and processed by our gut. These concepts may seem pedantic, but thinking through them is the first step towards creating an incentive to apply the discipline needed to cultivate integrity of our bodies and minds. Mental health is probably the single most important factor in maintaining a healthy perspective and mindset that will most favor our deepest intentions.

Building integrity of character sounds noble. However, it is the best way for us to take responsibility for ourselves in the fabric of humanity of which we are a part. It also creates the least amount of self-created resistance towards our objectives, meaning we can spend our time and energy being our most authentic selves instead of trying to maintain different versions and varieties of ourselves that we may create to serve different people and contexts. In that sense, integrity only holds strong when practiced with consistency. We can also practice modeling the characteristics that we would like to see in others.

We may all define integrity of character in different ways, but for me, it's treating others with respect as a default and favoring degrees of openness, honesty, and vulnerability appropriate to the level of trust that's been established. Furthermore, for those whom I truly care for and hold dear, in any context, I have a rule for myself to prioritize care for them to my fullest ability when in interaction with them. That concept in action usually means approaching a person or situation with humility; realizing that we may know very little and that the most important thing may be to first hold space and listen, with an open mind and heart.

Trust is the glue that bonds humanity.

Integrity breeds trust, and from what I have experienced, true trust is established on a subconscious level. Just as we will trust a structure with integrity to best shelter us, by sheer feeling alone, we will also be more apt to trust those around us when we feel, deep inside of us and without even thinking about it, that they have good integrity. Moreover, our work on our own integrity develops deeper trust in ourselves. If we accept the premise that modern life mostly exists in a fabric of humanity in which we are a part, then it's important to consider what attributes create the greatest potential for a well-functioning human relationship. I believe the single greatest attribute is trust. Trust creates the strongest foundation of connection in any context: business, love, friendships, and even family. Trust is also delicate, highlighting again the full consistency needed for our integrity to be true.

Shifting perspective.

In that moment when I felt that so much of what defined me, my relationship, and my job, suddenly disappeared, I watched my reality collapse. But I quickly realized that my reality was purely based on my perspective, and that my perspective was locked in, emotionally, to my expectations around others. And those others have their own agency, their own expectations, and their own perspectives that may or may not include me. I found the opportunity to extract those expectations and find the responsibility that I have to myself. I looked inward to my own integrity; to who I am in the world when I am all that I have and can count on in this world. And from my center, I decided to shift. I shifted away from a perspective and reality that included expectations that I had built around people that I no longer had access to in my life. I took the opportunity to look and think deeper, to realize that I had a blank slate from which I could build a new perspective, a new reality, and with a deep humility towards the unknown, a new perspective began to emerge.

I would like to take time to acknowledge that in these moments, I was also feeling a great deal of emotional pain. In fact, even now, almost a year later, I am still dealing with and working through much of that pain. Our emotions are so powerful, and as much as we would like to use reason and logic to direct our emotions, they are on their own slow schedule. This is how we are and how it should be. There is a danger when feeling this pain and the depression and/or anxiety that may follow, where we may decide, consciously or unconsciously, to ignore or bury this pain away. I'd encourage anyone to do their best not to do this, to instead feel their feelings. This may require help, and I am a very strong advocate for therapy if that option is available. In fact, I am back seeing my own therapist after an 11-year break as I want to give myself as much support as I can to process everything that makes up my emotions.

The Alchemy of Art.

At this very moment, I turned to another method of emotional processing, expressive art. I was acting at this time, for fun, with a local neighborhood theater group, Zombie Joe's Underground in North Hollywood, CA. When I had acted in my first play with them, *Urban Death: Tour of Terror*, a year prior, my best friend, Shannon Wong, saw me and expressed a strong desire to do the same. She told me that she would not only like to act, but also sing onstage. As a lifelong hobbyist musician, I told her that I would write something for her one day. That thought entered my mind again, and I figured that this would be the best time to make good on my promise. I wasn't a playwright; not yet, and had never written a complete story as an adult, but I figured I didn't have much more to lose.

I was about to play co-lead as a supervillain (and two other roles) in a superhero parody-comedy called *The Guy Man & Maureen*, written by Dirk Voetberg. The third of three plays in a row where I had been cast as a co-lead, this one was as a favor to cover for another actor who had dropped from the project. It was August 23rd, our opening night, and that day I fell ill with the worst food poisoning that I'd ever experienced in my life. I remember showing up to the theater for our pre-show run-through, and I was unable to stand up. I laid on the floor reciting my lines while the other actors worried as to whether the show would go on. I told them not to worry. This was a new play, never seen before, and I knew that the audience had no expectations. No matter what I was able to do that evening, the audience would accept it "as written." This came from understanding the perception of the audience, which was their reality, and the humility that enabled me to do whatever it took to fulfill their expectation, no matter how badly I may look in the process.

But somehow, the moment I appeared on stage as the narrator of act one, uttering the first words of the play, I was able to perform without too much of a problem. After the performance, in my post-performance and mid-illness delirium (it took me 7 more days, which included 2 more performances, to fully recover), I approached Zombie Joe, the theater owner, and asked him if I could produce and direct my own play at the theater. He not only said yes, but immediately set a date for the play's premiere. It would be January 10th and would be the theater's first production of 2025. I quickly realized that what enabled and drove him to so quickly support me in my proposal was a deep trust that we had established from my integrity in our work together, not only throughout the past year, but that very evening.

After we spoke, I went home and took the next couple of weeks, while recovering and performing, to paint a poster for *Soulmate* using a novel workflow, the details of which were published in an article that I wrote for the March 2025 issue of *Fenix Innovation Magazine*, released by the very same publisher of this book. With that poster announced in the press and on Zombie Joe's website, we started selling tickets. With tickets selling, I informed Shannon that her starring role was about to materialize (her reaction was initially "Are you joking? No," but I helped her to find her confidence…), and I started writing my play. Feeling the pressure of the upcoming premiere date, the tickets already being purchased, and the commitment I made to Zombie Joe to open his theatre's production year, I used my fears of each unknown ahead as my guide.

I shifted my perspective from a romantically fulfilled tech executive into that of a lonely heart, expressive romantic creative with a large well of emotion and thought to draw upon. I finished my script, wrote and recorded some music for Shannon to sing over, and with the guidance of Zombie Joe, cast and rehearsed *Soulmate*. Shannon was even able to contribute to the creative elements of the play by writing her own lyrics and vocal melodies. She had never done so before, but had always dreamed of being creative in that way. I think she was able to use me as an example of following her fears to take responsibility for her own dreams and become the artist that no one else around her expected.

Soulmate did open a day late, on January 11th instead of January 10th, due to the fires raging throughout Los Angeles. In fact, the morning of the 11th, one of my actors quit. In about 9 hours, I was able to move another actor into that now vacant role, rewrite the role that actor was playing to simplify the lines (they were too wordy), find a new actress, have her rehearse, run through the play with the cast, and have the most perfect opening evening with what turned out to be exactly the right cast and script.

Soulmate quickly drew in sold-out crowds. The raw expression of the play, which dealt with love and profound loss, created a catharsis for a community already feeling so much due to the fires raging around us. I also started to realize that I had changed. I had dived so quickly into all of the challenges of creating the entire play production, I hadn't given myself time to reflect on the art's profound effect on our audience. Many people would find themselves laughing throughout, and crying at the end. Many people spoke with me after the performance, sharing that they felt the authenticity of the piece and asked about the pain I had suffered. They shared their own stories of loss and expressed an appreciation for experiencing a performance that was unafraid of exploring some of our deepest sources of our own torment. I was asked some very direct questions about my own experience and how it showed up in the play. I realized, with humility and through the audience's perspective, that so much of my deepest emotional processes in dealing with my own loss were showing up on the stage; and that I was alchemizing my own pain, through art, into a shared healing.

Soulmate 1st-run Cast and Crew (from left to right: Raven Mahoney, Kyle Donovan, Charlotte Cocker, Steven Arce, Jorge Vaca, Shannon Wong, Michael Silva, Sunn'e Ratcliff, Douglas Clarke, Nena Martins, Zombie Joe), Zombie Joe's Underground Theatre - North Hollywood, CA

After the success of the extended Los Angeles run, a deep and spontaneous feeling hit me, telling me that I should take the production to what was my home before Los Angeles: New York City. I shared this feeling with Zombie Joe, who (unbeknownst to me) had, in the past, taken some of his own productions to New York. He was incredibly supportive and very quickly introduced me to one of his mentors, Edmund Gaynes. With Zombie Joe's recommendation, Ed immediately offered me the opportunity to take *Soulmate* Off-

Broadway, and it officially opened at his Actors' Temple Theatre in Manhattan's theater district on April 19th, 2025 (after two successful previews).

Moving to New York City to create an Off-Broadway show, casting mostly local New York theater talent, was the greatest perspective shift of all. To help document the journey, I created and started publishing "The Soulmate Podcast." In interviews with the LA and NYC cast, and parts of the production team, I offer transparent feelings and processes, in real time, as I reshape myself into someone I am discovering along with everyone watching and listening.

After one extension, Soulmate's Off-Broadway run ended on June 25th. I came home on June 27th and immediately got to work writing this chapter. I hope my experience and the sharing of the tools I developed and used to approach this present moment are helpful to you, the reader, and I look forward to seeing where our fears lead us next. Only by stepping into the unknown can we learn something entirely new.

Soulmate Off-Broadway Extension Cast (from left to right: Jaque Jeanne, Kolter Yagual-Rolston, Sean Amato, Nicolette Boillotat, Douglas Clarke, Avery Baxter, Shannon Wong, Sunn'e Ratcliff, Georg Jansen),
Actors Temple Theatre - New York, NY

Jackie Goodman

Lifestyle Leadership Coach & Balance Strategist
Redefining Success for High Achievers

www.linkedin.com/in/jackie-goodman
https://www.facebook.com/jackiegoodman01/
www.jackiegoodman.co.uk

Jackie Goodman is a UK-based, award-winning, globally accredited Senior Practitioner Coach through the EMCC (European Mentoring & Coaching Council), and well-being consultant. She is also a writer, speaker, successful entrepreneur, and former law firm partner. After breaking free from the burnout cycle as a high-performing lawyer, she rebuilt her life from the inside out—creating a business and lifestyle grounded in balance, well-being, and sustainability, not exhaustion. Today, Jackie passionately supports high achievers, senior professionals, and leadership teams in sectors from law to entrepreneurship, across the UK, Europe and beyond, who are ready to stop running on empty and build success that feels as good on the inside as it looks on paper. Drawing on what she's both lived and led through, Jackie's approach blends the empathy of someone who's been there with the clarity of someone who now lives what she teaches. She walks the talk of balanced success—finding joy in slow mornings with her rescue dogs and regular trips abroad. She also channels her success into supporting animal rescue organisations close to her heart. Jackie's work goes far beyond surface-level strategies. Whether supporting individuals or teams, she helps reset the deeper mindset patterns that keep people stuck in survival mode —shifting how they think, lead, and live. This chapter is an invitation to pause, reflect, and rethink what success could truly mean for you. So, grab a cuppa, get comfy... and read on._____________________

Rewriting Success: The Mindset Shift That Turns Balance into a Power Move

By Jackie Goodman

Introduction: You Don't Need to Escape Your Life—You Just Need to Rethink It

If you've ever felt outwardly successful but inwardly burned out, you're not alone. Rest assured, there is another way and, in this chapter, I'm going to share some of the ways you can start to move beyond the hamster wheel of constant busyness to feel back in control of your time, free yourself from punishing expectations, and feel more joy in your life—all without losing the success you currently enjoy.

In high-performance environments, it's easy to get caught in a cycle of striving, always pushing harder in the name of success, but for many, there comes a moment when the promotions, industry awards, and even professional status, stop feeling like a win. You're hitting the goals, but you're also running on empty. On the surface, everything looks impressive, but beneath it is exhaustion, depletion, and a persistent question: *Is this it?*

I know that feeling all too well. As a practising lawyer, I spent years in constant overdrive—high standards, voluminous caseloads, and relentless pressure. I believed that if I just kept pushing and climbing the ladder, I'd hit that ever-elusive jackpot of enjoying a happy work-life balance and finally 'smell the roses.' Unfortunately, the opposite was true. In law, the higher you climbed, the more pressure you took on, not just from the most complex caseloads, but from leadership challenges thrown into the mix.

Drinking too much to 'unwind' was a common trait amongst busy professionals. Well-being came second to performance. Weekends were usually spent working or trying to recharge. By Monday morning, I was already exhausted. I was constantly recovering from the very life I had worked so hard to create, and realising that was devastating.

You might be able to relate to this. On paper, it appeared I was thriving. I loved the law and was good at it. I hit targets (often exceeded them) and made Partner. I was seen as capable and successful. But inside, I was conflicted and struggling. The lack of control over my time left me feeling trapped. What I truly craved wasn't just professional success, but a deeper sense of balance and freedom—a way to thrive in my work without it taking over my life.

For years, I tried to ignore that ever-growing feeling and just kept going. Everyone around me seemed to be under the same pressure. I convinced myself it was normal.

Over time, I noticed the quiet toll it was taking, not just on me. I saw exceptional, dedicated colleagues pushed to the brink. I witnessed burnout, health issues, strained relationships—even, tragically, suicide. These weren't isolated incidents. They were symptoms of a culture that prioritised output over wellbeing, and of a version of success we all unknowingly internalised.

Then in 2012, everything changed. On top of the relentless pace of the job, I faced a series of personal challenges that forced me to take some time off. But that space gave me something I hadn't felt in years—perspective. With that came a bold decision: to step away from legal practice and start building a different kind of life.

I moved into the entrepreneurial world and built a business on my own terms, one designed not just for financial results, but for the kind of balance and freedom I had long been craving. What started as a practical step soon turned into something far deeper. I immersed myself in the psychology of burnout, high performance, and the beliefs we unconsciously inherit about what success should look like.

Over time, I built a more aligned way of living and had the privilege of sharing these insights with leaders across diverse industries. Through that work, I witnessed a common thread: the same patterns of pressure and quiet depletion I had once known so well.

But I also discovered something else: a different way to lead—a much clearer, quieter, and more authentic way. Creating space, aligning with my values, and working differently opened the door to growth I hadn't thought possible.

By slowing down and working from a place of alignment, I found I was achieving more, not by doing more, but by thinking and leading differently. My work became more impactful, with more energy, clarity, and at a pace that's genuinely sustainable, not exhausting. The irony is that I'm achieving more now than I ever did when I was working crazy hours and constantly running on empty.

That journey crystallised what I had intuitively known all along:

1. **That success simply isn't truly success if it costs you your joy, your health, or your peace of mind, and**
2. **That true success must be built on a foundation that supports both ambition and well-being.**

I've been in the burnout trenches, and my journey has given me a unique understanding from both sides of the equation. I'm now passionate about helping high-achieving professionals and ambitious leaders across the entrepreneurial world, legal field, and other corporate sectors rethink their relationship with success.

It all starts with one powerful shift: openness to a different way of working and courage to let go of traditional definitions of success and the beliefs that perpetuate them. This isn't about quitting your job or walking away from ambition. It's about **rewiring the belief that success requires exhaustion** and challenging the story we've inherited—that our value is linked to hours burned on the job, and rest is a reward rather than a power move.

This chapter is about shifting the mindset that keeps us trapped in cycles of overwork, burnout, and disconnection from our truth and values. It's about reconnecting with what matters most, challenging beliefs that no longer serve us, and building a version of success that fits who we truly are, not just on paper, but in real life.

In the pages ahead, I'll share some of the mindset shifts, coaching tools, and leadership insights that have helped me—and the high achievers I work with—move from burnout to balance.

The Old Success Story: Why Do We Do It to Ourselves?

Why do so many incredibly intelligent and talented people keep running themselves into the ground, even when it's clearly not good for their health, relationships, or mental well-being? In my experience, it usually comes down to two things: the culture around us and the mindset within us. I'll touch on culture here, but it's the inner wiring I'll go deeper into.

Workplace Culture

As I've shared, in my earlier professional life, I absorbed the belief that success and balance can't coexist, that one must be sacrificed for the other. We unconsciously 'collect' such beliefs as we go through life, often from an early age. For many high achievers, it's the norm for progress to come at a cost. We're taught that if we're not busy, we're not valuable, and that achievement means constantly pushing ourselves harder.

This is reinforced when promotions are given to those who 'live and breathe' their work, who stay late, arrive early, and rarely take breaks. I've even heard whispers of 'part-timer' to people logging off at 5 p.m., or someone starting at 9 a.m. being frowned at by those who had been bashing away since 7 a.m., with flippant quips like, "Afternoon, nice of you to drop in!"

Sadly, in too many business environments, exhaustion is still mistaken for drive—seen not as a red flag, but as proof of commitment. This is why I'm passionate about working with organisations to help them create a healthier workplace that encourages a balanced approach to work and understands the benefit of looking after top talent.

Let me be clear, there's no blame—or shame—here. Most leaders who perpetuate unhealthy cultures were shaped by the same system themselves and are often just repeating what they were taught. So, if you're either a leader who recognises any of this, or a high achiever working within this type of culture, be kind to yourself, but be open to the possibility of a different way.

The Mindset Behind the Madness

Whilst there's no denying that some of the problem stems from the cultural expectations in many workplaces, it's not just culture—we often carry beliefs that keep us pushing, even when no one's asking us to.

I've seen countless entrepreneurs, with no boss setting deadlines and no colleagues to compete against, still work themselves into exhaustion. What's clear is that much of what fuels burnout doesn't come from external pressure alone; it comes from within. Hidden scripts, beliefs, and buried fears shape how we show up, even when some part of us instinctively knows something needs to change.

i) **Where Those Beliefs Begin: The Lies We Learn About Worth**

When we spend years in systems like schools, sports clubs, and workplaces where performance and competition are embedded, it's little wonder we unconsciously absorb subtle but powerful messages about what makes us valuable. Over time, those beliefs harden into an invisible rulebook:

- Productivity = worth
- Rest = laziness
- Busyness = status

Eventually, these rules become internalized. You stop seeing rest as a necessity and start seeing it as a weakness. You feel guilty when you're not being *'useful'*. You begin measuring your value by how much you're doing, not how impactful you're being. After my corporate years, it took real effort to allow myself to pause without feeling guilty or lazy.

Here's the truth: ***Your value has never depended on output,*** but when your identity has been built around constantly excelling, slowing down can be confronting. So, we keep going, not because it's intentional or strategic, but because it's familiar. In those moments, it's hidden beliefs and habits that drive us.

We can often hear when hidden beliefs are at play, especially in the language people use. For example, how many times have you heard someone say, "I'm *soooo* busy!" They say it almost with a sense of pride, like it's proof, even to themselves, that they're working hard enough. Think of the typical question we ask each other, "How's work? Are you keeping busy?" Imagine feeling comfortable replying with, "Actually, no...I'm working efficiently on the right things to hit my goals *and* enjoy a great lifestyle." Wouldn't it be fabulous if *that* was the goal—endorsed and encouraged by work culture?

To change how we experience success, we must *rewire the mindset silently driving it*, because if we don't understand what's driving us, we can't consciously choose a different direction.

I recently worked with a client who, through coaching, realised she was 'addicted' to busyness and felt she had no use if she wasn't in service, both at work and at home. We unpacked this and rebuilt a much healthier (and kinder) belief, enabling her to take moments, *just for herself*. It was uncomfortable for her at first, but she's building on this week by week and finding joy in her work again.

So, let's look at some of the ways to recognize when your mindset needs a reset, identify the beliefs keeping you constantly pushing, and, as importantly, help you reclaim calm and clarity without abandoning your goals.

Take a moment here: grab a cuppa and a notepad, sit somewhere quiet and ask yourself...

- *What did I learn about productivity and achievement growing up?*
- *What belief is driving my current pace?*
- *Have I linked my worth to how busy or in control I appear?*
- *Whose definition of success am I living by? Is it serving me?*
- *If nobody was watching—and there was no social media—what would success look like for me?*

ii) The Inner Critic That Keeps You Performing

Behind high-functioning burnout is often a relentless inner critic—a voice so familiar it feels like truth. Again, no shame here; most of us know that voice well.

It cuts through your inner knowing, overriding the quiet signal that something's not right. Your body might be signalling it's time to stop, and a deeper part of you might be screaming out for rest, but that voice drowns it out and demands more.

This is the voice that tells you you're lazy for taking a break, that time off is indulgent, and that slowing down is failing. It dismisses your exhaustion and makes you question your resilience with unkind and unhelpful statements such as:

"You should be able to handle this."
"If you slow down, you'll fall behind."
"Other people are managing—what's wrong with you?"

This voice feeds off comparison, guilt, and impossibly high standards. It convinces you that your worth lies in your productivity, that needing rest is weakness, and that the only way to be valuable is to stay visible, busy, ahead of others, and always in control. Over time, it creates a pattern where all your energy is spent proving yourself to others—and to yourself.

The danger is this: if left unchecked, it embeds itself as your truth. It runs on autopilot, keeping you operating far beyond your physical, emotional, and psychological limits. Under those circumstances, it's easy to see how burnout quietly takes hold. Often, it's hidden behind those who seem to be handling everything best, but are crumbling inside.

So, what can we do?

The goal here is to understand where the voice came from, learn to recognise it, challenge its messages, and reconnect with the part of you that knows another way is possible. When we hear the voice, we can pause, thank it for the reminder, then consciously and intentionally choose a healthier message, like: ***self-care is strategic, not selfish***.

Here's how one client described the impact of making this shift:

> *"Your coaching has empowered me to become a more effective and compassionate Practice Manager. By taking care of myself, I can better support and nurture my team, ultimately leading to a more positive and productive work environment."*
> – M.D.P. (Law Firm)

Reflection Prompt

Take a moment here. Think of a recent time when you felt overwhelmed, overextended, or pressured to keep going, even when something inside you was screaming for a break.

Now ask yourself:

- ***What was my inner dialogue?***

  Write down the exact words or tone. Was it urgent, critical, or dismissive? Capture it; this helps you spot it next time.

- ***Where might that voice come from?***

  Can you trace it to an experience, family value, former boss, or cultural message?

- ***What could I say to myself instead?***

  What would a kinder voice say? Something that honours your body's call for rest and reminds you that your worth isn't tied to output.

- ***What would shift if I treated myself with compassion?***

  What could change if you gave yourself permission to pause, or ask for what you need?

Take your time. Often, the most powerful mindset shifts begin not with a dramatic change, but with a single honest question. Sit quietly and observe what comes up—that's your truth emerging.

iii) Neuroscience: The Case for Rest and The Power of a Pause

When you've been operating on overdrive for too long, it's not just your energy that suffers—it's your brain.

It is widely documented that chronic stress can cause structural and functional changes in the brain, affecting cognitive function, emotional regulation, and overall mental well-being. The brain shifts into survival mode, making it harder to think clearly.

When this happens, we become reactive, less patient, and more prone to decision fatigue. We are less able to focus, and even small tasks can feel overwhelming. At this stage, we are on the brink of serious burnout.

This is why burnout can be so debilitating. From the outside, you seem to be coping and functioning normally, but inside, your reserves are dangerously low. Without an intentional pause, your brain never gets the signal that it's safe to slow down.

You can't produce your best work, make good decisions, or lead a team effectively when your nervous system is stuck in survival mode. I know this from experience. I've pushed myself beyond safe limits, but I've since learned a better way. I've seen the power of stopping, taking a break, and regrouping, not just in my own businesses.

Helen, a busy team leader in a Law Firm, recognised her need to slow down:

"With Jackie's support, I've adapted my management and leadership style so that I take more breaks, which has made me more reflective and strategic in my approach."

It starts with a decision—to trust that giving yourself space leads to better results than pushing through. That single act of trust gives your brain a chance to recalibrate and helps you shift from survival into sustainability.

It's not easy to do when facing deadlines, but the pause becomes your power move. If you're open to making this change, it will pay dividends for your health, wellbeing, happiness, family life, and financial results.

iv) The Delegation Mindset: Why Letting Go Is a Leadership Strength

Delegating effectively is an art, but this isn't a 'how-to' on delegation. It's about something deeper—shifting the mindset behind our need to hold on, even when we know we should be letting go.

In coaching, I often see brilliant leaders who are overwhelmed, not because they're incapable, but because they're trying to do too much themselves. They often become the bottleneck in their own team or business.

Do you resonate with this?

See if any of this sounds familiar:

"It's quicker if I just do it."
"They won't do it as well as I will."
"I don't have time to explain it."
"It'll just come back wrong, so I might as well do it myself!"

On the surface, these sound practical and logical. It can feel quicker to just do it rather than explain it to someone else. The problem is, over time, this creates an over-reliance on you, keeps you from focusing on more important tasks, and leaves your team underutilised and increasingly disengaged.

Why do we do it?

Often, it's several things: fear of letting go, a need to control, perfectionism, lack of confidence in others, or simply not knowing how to delegate effectively.

But here's what I've seen time and time again: when a leader shifts their mindset around letting go, everything changes. Space opens to lead effectively, energy returns, and confidence grows, in themselves and in others.

Take Raj, a senior legal professional. For years, he equated success with doing it all and never showing vulnerability. That left him drained and self-critical.

Through coaching, he began to redefine success. He let go of the belief that leadership meant doing everything alone. He started delegating more, leading with calm, and showing up with greater clarity and purpose.

*"I've been given the help to develop strong leadership
skills, empowering me to motivate and guide my team
effectively—to delegate, provide feedback, and inspire."*
– Raj, Legal Leader

Let's pause here for some honest reflection.

1. Ask Yourself: Are You the Bottleneck?

Over the next few days, notice when you think or say things like:

- *"I'll just do it."*
- *"It's easier (or quicker) if I handle it."*

Write it down without judgement. This isn't about fixing the habit overnight; it's about noticing where you might be creating avoidable pressure on yourself that could be shared.

2. Now Reflect:

- What belief lies beneath your hesitation to delegate?
- What might be fuelling it? (e.g., fear, perfectionism, past experiences)
- What might shift if you saw letting go as leadership, not loss or weakness?

3. Next, Reframe the Belief:

Example:
Old belief: *"No one can do it like I can."*
New belief: *"Letting go is how I grow, and how I help others grow, too."*

Next time you notice yourself holding on, consciously state your new belief out loud, pass the task on, and notice how your confidence builds. If you experience resistance, start with something small—a low-stakes task—and give yourself the chance to practice letting go. Every time you do, you reinforce a new, more empowered way of leading.

Practical Shifts for Sustainable Success

i) Time Boundaries and the Mindset That Sabotages Them

One of the most important shifts I help clients make is seeing their time as valuable.

We often protect meetings or events involving others but allow constant interruptions to the time we've carved out for thinking, planning, or working on complex matters that need our full focus.

If you don't protect your time, no one else will. We teach others how to treat us, and when our boundaries are weak, people will interrupt us, often forcing us to cut into our family time to play catch-up with our work. That's a well-worn path to frustration, depletion, and burnout. When you honour your time, you model a more productive, sustainable way of working, not just for yourself, but for others.

Despite this, I see many leaders resisting the idea of setting clear boundaries around their time, often due to underlying beliefs, like:

- *"I should always be available."*
- *"I don't want to seem rude."*
- *"If I don't respond quickly, I'll let someone down."*

But there needs to be a mindset shift here—from feeling that by protecting your time, you're being selfish or letting your team down, to understanding that real leadership is about creating working patterns that set a better example.

Without challenging them, these beliefs will continue to sabotage your ability to do the deep, focused work in shorter timeframes, which is essential to a healthy work-life balance.

Mindset Reframe

Old belief: *"I need to be available to be valuable."*

New belief: *"Boundaries protect the quality of my leadership, and my life."*

Practice: Protect a Power Hour

- Block 60 minutes daily for thinking, deep work, planning, or decompressing.
- Label it clearly: *"CEO Hour,"* or *"Creative Focus."*
- Turn off notifications. Close the door. Treat it like a meeting with someone important—because it is!

If someone tries to interrupt, avoid over-explaining. Try this simple response: *"I'm in focused work mode, I'll check back shortly."*

Remember, every time you say yes to an interruption, you teach others that your boundaries are flexible, and you say no to what matters more.

One client—a team leader in a large law firm—called this a "game-changer."

Out of habit and fear of letting others down, she'd made herself constantly available, which left her exhausted and resentful. Through coaching, she began protecting her time and regained her composure. Contrary to her fears, her team respected her more and followed her example. Interruptions reduced, tensions eased, and overall productivity improved.

ii) Environment Shapes Energy - Set Yourself Up for Flow

Mindset matters, but your environment amplifies it.

Your environment is never neutral. It either supports clarity, focused thinking, and calm, or it adds friction, stress, and noise.

If you're trying to make important decisions from a cluttered kitchen table, a messy desk, or a noisy open-plan office, your brain is already working overtime. When you're in strategic or high-value work mode, you want your attention fully on the task.

I once worked in a noisy open-plan office and found it difficult to focus. When trying to read key statements, I'd re-read the same sentence multiple times. I had to get creative just to find quiet spaces, sometimes even sitting on the stairwell at the top of the building.

Don't underestimate the impact of your environment. When you create spaces for deep thinking, you often get the task done faster, freeing up time and energy to switch off sooner and enjoy life beyond your desk.

Small shifts can help. Try designating one clean, distraction-free space for high-value work. Your mind will begin to associate that space with focus. I also use music to train my mind into deep focus: classical or spa music helps me write, plan, or think strategically. Experiment and find what works for you.

Shift Your Scene to Shift Your State

Whilst having an uncluttered workspace is important, sometimes we need a complete change of scenery to unlock an entirely new mindset.

When clients feel stuck in a loop, or mentally foggy, I don't ask, "*What* are you thinking?"

I ask, "*Where* are you thinking?"

When my thinking feels stale, I take my laptop or journal to a quiet hotel lounge or my garden retreat. A change in ambience often brings the clarity that eluded me at my desk.

One client had spent days going round in circles over a complex business challenge. Just by stepping away and taking a notepad to a peaceful park, the answer came to her in less than 15 minutes. The problem hadn't changed, but the new setting changed her energy and sparked new ideas.

The goal here isn't to work more. It's to work better in short, focused sessions that support a balanced, sustainable life *without* compromising your drive or results. It's worth remembering that the right environment doesn't just clear your mind, it fuels your focus.

Tool: Environment Reset

Use this simple practice to keep your physical space working *for* you, not against you.

1. Reflect:

- *Where have I spent most of my work time this week?*
- *How has that space affected my energy or focus?*

2. Reset:

- *What one small change could make that space more conducive to creative or high-value work?*

3. Reimagine:

- *What kind of environment brings out my best, and how can I use it more intentionally next week?*

Conclusion: Real Power Is a Clear Mind

Success doesn't have to cost your well-being. Balance isn't just some fluffy ideal; it's essential, and allows you to work efficiently, sustainably, and in a way that's rewarding and enjoyable. It keeps you fresh and motivated.

The alternative is frustration, overwhelm, burnout, and eventually the point where you either choose, or are forced, to walk away. What a shame and a waste of your incredible talent, or the talent of your team members who may crash and burn, undoing the years you've invested in their growth.

In this chapter, I've shared just a handful of the tools and mindset shifts that can help you rethink success and build a more sustainable way of working and leading.

I want to see us move away from outdated thinking to prioritise quality over quantity, and to redesign our working patterns in a way that supports both performance and well-being. It also means being honest and self-aware enough to recognise when we're in our own way, allowing us to let go of control, delegate effectively, set healthy boundaries, and lead by example.

Will we get it right every time? Of course not, but our most strategic tool is our willingness to **pause, reflect, and reset early**, before things unravel or old habits creep back in.

Speaking as someone who's come through it and built a business and a lifestyle on the other side, here's what I want you to take away:

Don't wait until you're forced to stop before you allow yourself to slow down.

You're allowed to define success on your own terms—in a way that supports your whole life, not just your business.

This isn't just mindset work. It's the foundation for a new way to lead and live.

And it's only the beginning.

It's the work I do every day with high-performing professionals who are done with burnout and ready to lead from clarity, strength, and sustainability. If you're ready to explore this further, I'd love to support you. Reach out to me at ***hello@jackiegoodman.co.uk***.

Success that costs you everything isn't really success, and **I believe, deeply, that balance isn't a luxury—it's a leadership strategy.**

With much love,

Jackie 🤍

Nikki Girard

Heart Energy X Me
Visionary Entrepreneur, Exponential Transformation &
Manifestation Expert, Strategic Business Development

https://www.linkedin.com/in/nikki-girard-962601207
https://www.facebook.com/nikki.girard.311
https://www.instagram.com/nikki.girard.311
https://highafadvantage.com/
Clubhouse Community:
https://www.clubhouse.com/house/high-af-advantage

Nikki Girard, a visionary, as a 4-time award winning entrepreneur and expert in exponential transformation, manifestation, and Neuro Transcendence, she's a 4-time—#1 Amazon & 4-time—#1 International bestselling author, podcast host & speaker. As CEO of Heart Energy X Me, she guides clients towards their full potential with over 40 years, guiding leaders & individuals to exponential transformation & abundance using neuroscience, psychology, unique coaching methodologies and more. A Force Awards awardee, Senior Level Executive Contributor & Awardee CREA Global Awards 2025—Brainz Magazine, and sought-after speaker, Nikki's groundbreaking High AF Advantage methodologies are making a lasting impact, positioning her as a pioneer and inspiration in the field. New Podcast coming ⏩ Called: "High AF Advantage" the podcast-Stay tuned for when it goes live. Shatter your money codes and reshape your reality, as you quantum leap into the life you desire and deserve.

Mindset Mastery: Harnessing the Power Within

By Nikki Girard

Welcome to Mindset Mastery, where you'll unlock your full potential and achieve extraordinary success.

"Realize deeply that the present moment is all you have."
— **Eckhart Tolle**

Join Nikki on a transformative journey of self-discovery, exploring neuro-transcendence, the subconscious mind, and the High AF Advantage.

Prepare to reshape your life and become your best self.

Together, we'll uncover the keys to resilience, growth, and unparalleled achievement.

Dive into the mysteries of the mind and interconnectedness, unlocking your incredible potential and embracing limitless possibilities.

Ready to Rock & Roll

Get ready to supercharge your life with Mindset Mastery, the ultimate guide to breaking through mental barriers and unleashing your full potential!

This revolutionary book is jam-packed with powerful strategies and real-world applications designed to rewire your brain, skyrocket your confidence, and propel you towards extraordinary success.

Join an elite community of trailblazers who are reshaping the landscape of leadership and personal development.

When you master your mindset, you hold the key to a brighter, bolder, and more fulfilling future!

Emotional Intelligence: Increase Brain Power Potential

Emotions play a crucial role in our cognitive performance and overall well-being.

Developing emotional intelligence is essential in effectively managing our emotions and leveraging them to enhance our brain's potential.

Emotional intelligence involves four main components: self-awareness, self-management, social awareness, and relationship management.

By improving these skills, we can better navigate our emotional landscape, enabling us to stay focused, make better decisions, and foster stronger connections with others.

Research suggests that emotional intelligence has a significant impact on cognitive functions such as memory, problem-solving, and creativity.

As we become more attuned to our emotions, we can harness the power of positive emotional states, such as happiness, curiosity, and enthusiasm, to boost our mental performance and overall potential.

To cultivate emotional intelligence, practice the following strategies:

1. ***Develop Self-Awareness***

By noticing and acknowledging your emotional states.

2. ***Practice Self-Regulation Techniques***

Deep breathing or mindfulness can help manage your emotions more effectively.

3. ***Cultivate Empathy and Understanding***

Development of your emotional state and of others' emotions, enhancing your social awareness.

4. *Strengthen Relationship Management Skills*

Practicing through active listening, clear communication, and conflict resolution.

By incorporating emotional intelligence into our personal growth journey, we not only improve our mental performance but also enrich our relationships and overall quality of life.

The Power of Energy: Aura, Biofield, and Personal Growth

Energy is a fundamental aspect of our existence, connecting our physical, emotional, and spiritual selves.

In the context of personal growth and mindset mastery, understanding the role of energy in our lives can be incredibly beneficial.

The aura

This, often described as an energy field surrounding the body, is believed to reflect our emotional and spiritual state.

By becoming more attuned to our aura and the energy it holds, we can gain valuable insights into our well-being and work towards greater balance and harmony.

The biofield or human energy field

This is thought to play a crucial role in our overall health and well-being.

By learning to harness and manipulate our biofield through practices such as meditation, visualization, or energy healing, and being in the present moment.

These are just a few ways we can tap into our inner power and promote healing and transformation.

As you strive for mindset mastery and unlocking your full potential, remember the power of energy.

Neuro-Transcendence: A Journey Beyond the Self

Imagine the potential for personal growth and resilience that lies within you, waiting to be unlocked.

Neuro-transcendence, also known as self-transcendence, invites you on a transformative journey beyond your self-concept to discover a deeper connection with the world around you.

In the realm of psychology, neuro-transcendence involves expanding your self-concept, fostering a sense of interconnectedness, and promoting well-being.

It is associated with increased resilience and personal growth, leading to a more profound sense of meaning and purpose in life.

Metaphysics takes us even further, guiding us toward understanding reality beyond the physical world and uniting with a higher power.

By harmonizing the heart and brain coherence with the Earth's resonance frequency, you can experience neuro-transcendence.

This is a powerful state of being that enhances your connection with nature, spirituality, and the very fabric of existence.

Neuro-transcendence holds the key to unlocking your true potential, providing you with the tools to cultivate resilience, experience personal growth, and embrace the beauty of interconnectedness.

Discover the science behind neuro-transcendence and learn practical techniques to achieve it.

This journey will positively impact all aspects of your life, expanding your mind, nourishing your soul, and transforming your perspective on reality.

Exploring Various Aspects of Neuro-Transcendence

1. *Expanding Consciousness*

Our journey begins by delving into the role of consciousness in transcending our perceived limitations.

By cultivating awareness and embracing mystical experiences, we open the door to a deeper understanding of our interconnectedness with the world around us.

As our consciousness expands, so too does our potential for growth and transformation.

2. *Scientific Perspectives*

Science has begun to unravel the mysteries of transcendence through cutting-edge research.

Brain imaging studies have revealed changes in neural activity associated with transcendent experiences, while psychological assessments highlight improvements in well-being and personal growth.

As we continue to explore this fascinating frontier, the implications for mental and physical health are nothing short of extraordinary.

3. *Spiritual and Philosophical Insights*

Ancient wisdom and modern philosophy offer invaluable insights into the nature of self-transcendence.

Spiritual traditions, such as Buddhism and Taoism, emphasize the dissolution of the ego and the cultivation of unity with the divine.

Similarly, philosophical movements like transcendentalism encourage introspection and contemplation as paths to self-discovery.

These diverse perspectives provide a rich tapestry of knowledge, guiding us towards transcendent living.

4. *Navigating Challenges and Misconceptions*

The path to transcendence is not without its obstacles. Misconceptions may lead some to dismiss the concept as esoteric or impractical, while others may encounter resistance to change or fear of the unknown.

By addressing these challenges and fostering open-mindedness, we can navigate the path to transcendence with greater clarity and confidence.

5. *Cultural and Societal Impacts*

As more individuals embrace the pursuit of transcendence, the ripple effects can be felt throughout society.

This collective shift has the potential to reshape our cultural values, emphasizing empathy, connection, and cooperation over competition and isolation.

By working together to foster transcendent experiences, we can create a more harmonious and interconnected world.

Embarking on the Journey Towards Self-Transcendence: Ways & Tips

1. *Embrace Nature*

Spend time outdoors, immersing yourself in the natural world to foster peace and interconnectedness.

2. *Align Chakras*

Engage in practices such as meditation, yoga, or energy work to balance your chakras and encourage free-flowing energy.

3. *Listen to Music*

Tune into music that resonates with you, allowing it to evoke emotions and create a harmonious inner environment.

4. ***Pursue Enjoyable Hobbies***

Engage in activities that bring you joy and a sense of flow, whether it's cooking, playing sports, or engaging in creative pursuits.

5. ***Live in the Present Moment***

Practice mindfulness and conscious breathing to ground yourself in the now, facilitating a more balanced approach to life's challenges.

Personal Benefits of Self-Transcendence

Transcendence, both in terms of self-transcendence and its application to career and business, offers numerous personal benefits.

By embracing interconnectedness and unity, individuals can foster a more empathetic and resilient mindset, enabling them to navigate life's challenges with grace.

Practicing transcendence also encourages self-discovery, allowing individuals to align their personal values with their goals and find deeper meaning in their daily lives.

Furthermore, maintaining work-life balance becomes more attainable, promoting overall well-being and satisfaction.

Career and Business Advantages

Incorporating transcendent practices into career and business environments can have a profound impact.

It enhances communication, boosts creativity, and improves productivity, creating a thriving and harmonious workplace.

Leaders who demonstrate transcendent qualities inspire trust and commitment, leading to organizational growth and success.

On an individual level, professionals can leverage transcendence to discover their true potential, aligning their personal and professional aspirations for increased fulfillment and purpose in their careers.

By integrating these practices into your daily routine, you'll create a solid foundation for exploring and experiencing the transformative power of self-transcendence.

Mindset Mastery: Brain Rewiring, Influence, and Overcoming Limiting Beliefs

Tapping Inner Potential: The Subconscious Frontier

Nestled within our brainstem lies the reticular formation, a network of neurons that plays a crucial role in controlling our level of consciousness, attention, and sensory processing.

Known as the reticular brain, this region functions as a cognitive filter, selecting and prioritizing information from our environment to determine what we perceive and focus on.

By understanding the workings of the reticular brain, we can harness its power to optimize our attention, enhance our cognitive abilities, and promote overall performance.

Key Functions of the Reticular Brain

1. *Attentional Filtering*

The reticular brain filters the countless stimuli we encounter daily, deciding what information reaches our conscious awareness and what gets ignored.

This filtering mechanism helps us maintain focus and avoid sensory overload.

2. *Arousal and Consciousness*

The reticular brain plays a vital role in controlling our arousal and alertness levels, influencing our sleep-wake cycles and overall energy.

3. *Habituation*

The reticular brain helps us adapt to recurring stimuli by reducing our response to them over time.

This process, known as habituation, allows us to conserve mental energy and prioritize novel or important information.

The Reticular Brain: Mastering Your Cognitive Filter

To tap into the power of your reticular brain, consider the following strategies:

1. *Mindfulness and Meditation*

Mindfulness practices can enhance your ability to focus, improve mental clarity, and regulate your arousal levels.

Regular meditation can also optimize the functioning of your reticular brain and strengthen neural pathways related to attention and cognitive control.

2. *Set Clear Intentions and Goals*

By clearly defining your goals and intentions, you prime your reticular brain to prioritize information and opportunities that align with your desired outcomes.

3. *Engage in Cognitively Stimulating Activities*

Challenging your brain with new experiences and learning opportunities promotes neuroplasticity and strengthens your reticular brain's filtering capabilities.

Incorporating these strategies into your daily life can help you leverage the power of your reticular brain.

When you unlock your untapped brain power potential, you can achieve optimal cognitive performance.

Unleashing the Power Within: Exploring the 95% Untapped Brain Power Potential

The human brain is a remarkable organ, capable of incredible feats of intelligence, creativity, and problem-solving.

Yet, it is believed that we only utilize a fraction of its true potential.

The 95% Untapped Brain Power Potential

This concept invites us to explore the vast capabilities that lie dormant within us.

At the core of this concept is the understanding that our brain possesses immense untapped resources.

While we may be familiar with our conscious thoughts and actions, the majority of our brain's activity occurs beneath the surface.

In the realm of the subconscious mind, it is estimated that only about 5% of our cognitive processes are conscious, leaving a staggering 95% untapped potential waiting to be unleashed.

Exploring the untapped potential of our brain begins with expanding our awareness and understanding of its inner workings.

We delve into the realms of neuroscience, psychology, and consciousness, seeking insights into the hidden depths of our cognitive abilities.

We learn about the power of neuroplasticity, the brain's ability to reorganize and form new neural connections, and how we can harness this potential for personal growth and transformation.

To tap into this untapped potential, we engage in practices that stimulate and activate our brain's latent abilities. We embrace lifelong learning, challenging ourselves to acquire new knowledge and skills.

We engage in activities that promote mental agility, such as puzzles, brain games, and creative pursuits.

We explore meditation and mindfulness practices that enhance our ability to focus, reduce stress, and tap into our intuition and creativity.

The untapped potential of our brain also lies in the realm of our subconscious mind.

By accessing and reprogramming our subconscious beliefs and patterns, we can unlock new levels of success, happiness, and fulfillment.

Techniques such as visualization, affirmations, and hypnosis can help us tap into this vast reservoir of untapped potential, allowing us to overcome limitations and achieve our goals.

As we embark on this journey of exploring the 95% untapped brain power potential, we must also cultivate a growth mindset.

We embrace the belief that our abilities and intelligence are not fixed but can be developed and expanded.

We let go of self-imposed limitations and embrace the idea that we are capable of continuous growth and improvement.

Unleashing the power within requires dedication, practice, and a willingness to step outside of our comfort zones.

It is a journey of self-discovery and self-mastery, where we unlock the full potential of our brain and tap into the limitless possibilities that await us.

So, let us embark on this exploration of the 95% untapped brain power potential, with curiosity and a sense of wonder.

Let us expand our awareness, engage in practices that stimulate our cognitive abilities, and reprogram our subconscious beliefs.

In doing so, we unlock the door to our true potential and create a life of limitless possibilities.

Mindset Mastery: Brain Rewiring, Influence, and Overcoming Limiting Beliefs

In this section, we delve into the transformative power of the subconscious mind's influence on mindset.

We are exploring strategies for brain rewiring, overcoming limiting beliefs, and harnessing the potential of a growth mindset.

By embracing the principles of Mindset Mastery, you'll unlock the potential within yourself and others, fostering resilience, empowerment, and incredible success.

Neuroplasticity-Unlocking and the Subconscious Mind

Neuroplasticity, the brain's remarkable ability to adapt and change in response to experiences and learning, plays a pivotal role in our personal growth and development.

By engaging in new experiences and practicing mindfulness, we can stimulate neuroplasticity, fostering a growth mindset.

Contrary to the once-held belief that the brain's structure and function were fixed after a certain age, neuroplasticity reveals the brain's incredible capacity to reorganize and form new neural connections throughout our lives.

This powerful mechanism allows us to shape our thoughts, emotions, and behaviors, ultimately influencing our mindset and overall well-being.

Our subconscious mind shapes our beliefs and behaviors. To transform our mindset, we must uncover subconscious patterns and reframe our internal narratives.

Embrace the power of mindset mastery by harnessing neuroplasticity, which empowers us to create lasting change and break free from self-limiting patterns.

By acknowledging the subconscious and committing to growth and dedication, you'll navigate life's challenges and create your desired reality.

Meet Nikki Girard: Creator of High AF Advantage—Unique Contribution to the Industry

Nikki Girard, a visionary entrepreneur, has made a significant impact on the coaching and personal development industry through her innovative approach and unwavering dedication to helping others reach their full untapped potential.

Her commitment to transformative change is exemplified by her development of the groundbreaking High AF Advantage program.

She combines cutting-edge neuroscience, psychology, coaching strategies, and energy engineering to empower individuals on their journey to success.

A two-time Executive Contributor for Brainz Magazine and recipient of the prestigious Brainz 500 Global List award, Nikki shares the spotlight with luminaries such as Oprah Winfrey, Marisa Peer, Jim Kwik, Jay Shetty, and Rachel Paling.

As the Founder and CEO of Heart Energy X Me, Nikki is a highly sought-after Quantum Resiliency Coach, helping clients build mental resilience and adaptability, and Strategic Business Consultant, guiding businesses to achieve sustainable growth and success.

With her own experiences of overcoming traumas and adversities fueling her passion, Nikki has devoted over 38 years to studying Human Behavior & Design, Consciousness, Subconscious Reprogramming, Energy & Meditation Techniques.

Her extensive knowledge and expertise in Hypnotherapy, Psychotherapy, Advanced Alternative Healing Modalities, Hermetic Principles, and other cutting-edge methodologies enable her to offer tailored solutions and provide life-changing results for her clients.

Embracing the Transformative Power of the High AF Advantage: Harnessing Your Full Potential

While many coaching methods emphasize the importance of 'stepping out of one's comfort zone' to achieve growth, Nikki Girard offers a refreshing alternative with her groundbreaking High AF Advantage approach.

Rather than pushing individuals beyond their limits, her method focuses on empowering them to 'step into their comfort zone,' fostering a sense of self-confidence and inner strength that propels them towards their highest aspirations and potential.

The **High AF Advantage** hinges on the strategic integration of four key pillars, coupled with the robust foundation provided by the Conscious Success Integration (C.S.I) Quantum Style fundamentals, and the dynamic force that is Quantum Flex.

Quantum Flex serves as the catalyst for transformation, embodying the limitless potential and possibilities that lie within each individual.

As the secret weapon that supercharges manifestation, Quantum Flex equips clients with the necessary tools to break through barriers and achieve extraordinary success and abundance.

Drawing on the adaptability and strength cultivated through **Quantum Flex**, individuals are empowered to make quantum leaps into their desired reality, harnessing the full potential of their intentions and desires.

Meanwhile, the ***Conscious Success Integration*** component acts as a unifying force, seamlessly binding the various elements of the High AF Advantage method into a cohesive whole.

Quantum Physics: Unlocking Limitless Potential

The science of quantum physics has unraveled profound truths about the nature of our universe, revealing that everything—from the largest galaxies to the tiniest subatomic particles—is composed of pure energy.

This discovery opens up boundless possibilities, as it suggests that our thoughts and emotions carry vibrational frequencies that interact with and influence our reality.

By understanding and harnessing these quantum principles, we can tap into the infinite potential of the universe and create profound transformations in our lives.

As we delve deeper into the world of mindset mastery, the insights offered by quantum physics become an essential guide.

It illuminates the path towards achieving our highest aspirations and unlocking our full potential.

Getting Out of the Matrix

Societal expectations can limit personal growth, as psychological studies reveal.

By breaking free from societal norms, we embrace self-actualization and explore our true potential.

> *"The Matrix is a system... That system is our enemy... You have to understand, most of these people are not ready to be unplugged. And many of them are so inured, so hopelessly dependent on the system, that they will fight to protect it."* — **Morpheus, The Matrix**

Maslow's hierarchy of needs emphasizes the importance of self-actualization, while Rogers' person-centered approach highlights the value of authenticity and individual growth.

Quantum Leap Into Your New Reality

Our mindset and intentions directly influence our future.

Neuroscience research demonstrates that visualization techniques activate similar neural pathways as physical actions, highlighting the power of thought in shaping reality.

> *"We are all energy. Energy can move in any direction.*
> *Use your energy to make an impact."* — **Jay Shetty**

This finding empowers us to leverage positive thinking and intention setting for transformative change.

> *"Imagination is more important than knowledge.*
> *Knowledge is limited. Imagination encircles the world."*
> — **Albert Einstein**

The Vortex

Entering a state of flow through energetic alignment helps achieve fulfillment and enhances manifestation abilities.

> *"When you are in alignment with the vortex, you are in*
> *alignment with your true power, and you are an*
> *unstoppable force."* — **Abraham Hicks**

Energy psychology research indicates that aligning thoughts, emotions, and actions creates a harmonious energy vortex, optimizing personal growth and success.

The Science Behind Mindset Mastery

Epigenetics and quantum mechanics illuminate the mind-body connection, contributing to our understanding of mindset mastery.

"Your mind can only think one thought at a time, so if you're thinking a positive thought, there's no room for a negative one." — **Marisa Peer**

Epigenetics explains how environmental factors and experiences influence gene expression, impacting well-being and behavior.

Quantum mechanics underscores the interconnectedness of all things, empowering individuals to tap into their limitless potential.

Understanding Resonance Frequency and Energy

Resonance frequency plays a crucial role in our personal energy and manifestation abilities.

It is the vibrational state at which we naturally resonate, influencing our thoughts, emotions, and experiences.

By understanding and aligning with our resonance frequency, we can tap into the quantum field of limitless potential and create our desired reality.

"If you want to find the secrets of the universe, think in terms of energy, frequency, and vibration."
— **Nikola Tesla**

The High AF Advantage recognizes the importance of resonance frequency in personal growth and transformation.

By raising our resonance frequency, we can attract positive experiences, enhance our intuition, and strengthen our manifestation abilities.

To achieve this elevated state, this encourages individuals to:

1. ***Cultivate Positive Thoughts and Emotions***

Focusing on gratitude, love, forgiveness, and joy.

2. ***Engage in Mindfulness Practices***

Practices such as meditation, visualization, and breathwork, to quiet the mind and connect with the present moment.

3. ***Embrace a Growth Mindset***

Continue learning and expanding our knowledge, skills, experiences, and growth.

4. ***Surround Ourselves with Support***

Surround yourself with people who are like-minded & uplifting individuals who inspire and encourage personal growth.

By incorporating these practices into our daily lives, we can increase our resonance frequency and align with the universal forces that govern manifestation and success.

This powerful synergy between intention, energy, and alignment enables us to tap into the quantum field and unlock our full potential.

This powerful fusion of techniques creates a launching pad for clients to embark on their journey towards unparalleled success and personal fulfillment.

Now that you understand the transformative power of the High AF Advantage and resonance frequency, take the next step in your personal growth journey.

Join Nikki as the host of <u>High AF Advantage-an Elite Exclusive</u> Clubhouse community and gain personalized insights and solutions to burning questions in Your Success Journey.

Join Nikki's New <u>Facebook Community</u> too.

Are you ready to embark on your own transformative journey?

Create Success-Impact-Legacy & book your complimentary <u>Quantum Clarity session with Nikki today</u> experience the power of neuro-transcending abundance firsthand!

Now let's dive in deeper...

The Four Key Pillars of the High AF Advantage

High AF Advantage is comprised of four interconnected pillars, each designed to cultivate different aspects of personal and professional development:

1. **Igniting Peak Brain Performance**

This pillar harnesses the power of neuroscience and neuroplasticity, offering strategies to optimize mental performance and unlock hidden potential.

2. **Flow State Sweet Spot**

By teaching individuals how to access a state of heightened focus and productivity, this pillar enables them to achieve more while maintaining a sense of balance and control.

3. **Cultivating Resilience**

Building the capacity to bounce back from challenges and adversity is essential for long-term success.

This pillar provides tools and techniques to develop emotional resilience and overcome obstacles with grace and determination.

4. **Self & Success Mastery**

The final pillar integrates the knowledge and skills developed in the previous three, as well as foundational fundamentals, to help individuals cultivate sustainable success, longevity, and personal fulfillment.

By addressing each of these essential areas, this offers a comprehensive and holistic approach to business growth and personal empowerment.

This enables individuals to create lasting positive change in their lives and careers.

Overcoming Entrepreneurial Challenges with the High AF Advantage

Entrepreneurs face unique challenges that demand resilience and adaptability. The High AF Advantage provides a robust toolkit to tackle these issues, focusing on essential aspects of business growth and success.

By spotting unproductive patterns, entrepreneurs can leverage the High AF Advantage to devise solutions and drive lasting success.

Be mindful of these patterns:

1. ***Procrastination and avoidance***

Struggling with these issues may lead to missed opportunities, strained relationships, and stagnant growth.

2. ***Rumination***

Overthinking can cause leaders to become paralyzed by indecision, affecting personal well-being and leading to missed opportunities.

3. ***Freezing or running***

Overwhelming stress may prevent individuals from showcasing their true potential in critical situations.

Internal Communication & Self-Talk

Negative self-talk undermines confidence and restricts risk-taking.

By leveraging the High AF Advantage pillars, entrepreneurs can conquer these challenges, promote growth, and secure lasting success in their ventures.

The High AF Advantage empowers entrepreneurs to break barriers, cultivate resilience, and fuel long-term success through innovation.

Personal Testimonials

To truly appreciate the transformative power of transcendence, we can turn to the inspiring stories of those who have experienced it firsthand.

Individuals from all walks of life have shared their personal accounts of overcoming adversity, finding meaning, and embracing interconnectedness.

To truly appreciate the transformative power and inspiring stories of those who experienced it firsthand, apply this revolutionary method.

Meet Ashley: The Mompreneur Coach & Best Selling Author

"Working with Nikki Girard has been a game-changer. Her seriously extensive knowledge and expertise make her a literal walking encyclopedia."

The "High AF Advantage" elite VIP 1-1 experience provides valuable insights and methodologies, and the integration process is literally seamless and easy.

Nikki's dedication to her clients' success is evident – she's there each step of the way. Connect with Nikki, and watch the transformation!"

Meet Hysam - Entrepreneur/Marketing

He praises Nikki Girard's deep understanding of the Quantum realm, he finds that he can balance his personal & Business life with ease, with laser focus, and in alignment. He continues to work toward higher aspirations.

His ability to resonate with each client, at their level and articulate what he brings to the table, catapulted his success and hit over $100,000 USD consistently!! And growing.

*He recommends the **"High AF Advantage" elite VIP 1-1 experience** for everyone looking to truly level up to **reach crazy abundance**.*

Visit highafadvantage.com for more information and inspiring testimonials from clients who have experienced the transformative power of the High AF Advantage.

With its innovative blend of neuroscience, psychology, and energy work, this method is poised to revolutionize the coaching industry.

Investing in Multidisciplinary Coaching: The Power of Expert Guidance

As you embark on your personal growth journey, consider the benefits of working with a multidisciplinary coach who can offer a holistic approach to your development.

A skilled coach, like Nikki Girard, can help you navigate the various aspects of mindset mastery, the High AF Advantage, and your overall well-being.

By investing in multidisciplinary coaching, you gain access to:

1. ***Customized guidance***

Tailored strategies and support based on your unique goals, strengths, and challenges.

2. *Diverse expertise*

A coach with a multidisciplinary background can offer insights from various fields, providing a well-rounded approach to your development.

3. *Accountability and motivation*

Regular coaching sessions help keep you focused, motivated, and accountable for your progress.

Working with a multidisciplinary coach can be an invaluable investment in your personal growth and success, offering expert guidance and support as you unlock your full potential.

Accelerating Your Progress: The Power of Expert Guidance

While personal growth is a journey that requires dedication and self-reflection, working with a skilled coach or mentor can significantly accelerate your progress.

By leveraging the expertise and experience of a multidisciplinary coach, you can:

1. *Avoid common pitfalls*

An experienced coach can help you navigate common obstacles and mistakes, saving you valuable time and energy.

2. *Receive personalized support*

Tailored coaching allows you to focus on areas that need the most attention, leading to more efficient and effective growth.

3. *Gain deeper insights*

A coach offers unique perspectives and insights, helping you uncover blind spots and deepen your understanding.

Investing in the right guidance transforms your personal growth journey from a slow, trial-and-error process to a streamlined path towards success.

With a knowledgeable and supportive coach, you can effectively harness and accelerate your progress.

Embracing the Journey: Overcoming Challenges and Staying Motivated

On your journey to Mindset Mastery, obstacles may arise. Maintain determination and resilience to overcome challenges.

Stay motivated by celebrating progress, seeking support, and focusing on why you started. Embrace the journey, trust the process, and commit to continuous growth.

Remember to keep in mind:

1. ***Reframe negative self-talk***

Challenge and replace limiting beliefs with empowering affirmations.

2. ***Seek support***

Surround yourself with positive influences and ask for help when needed.

3. ***Celebrate small wins***

Acknowledge and celebrate your achievements, no matter how small, to maintain momentum.

4. ***Focus on the long-term vision***

Keep your ultimate goals in mind, and don't become discouraged by temporary setbacks.

By embracing the journey, facing challenges head-on, and maintaining a growth mindset, you'll be well-equipped to achieve lasting success and unlock your full potential.

High AF Advantage: The New Coaching Revolution

The High AF Advantage, with its unique blend of neuroscience, psychology, and energy work, can be considered a game-changer in the industry.

By addressing the evolving needs and challenges faced by individuals and organizations, this method offers a comprehensive and holistic approach to personal and professional growth.

More people and businesses recognize the power of harnessing peak brain performance, accessing the flow state, cultivating resilience, and mastering self and success.

This is why the High AF Advantage will become an indispensable tool for anyone looking to thrive in an increasingly complex and competitive world.

In summary, the High AF Advantage represents the pinnacle of personal development, empowering individuals and organizations to achieve their full potential and reach new heights of success.

Place Your Cosmic Order: Unleash the Universe's Power for Extraordinary Success

Imagine a world where your wildest dreams are not just a distant possibility, but a reality waiting to be manifested.

This is the world of cosmic orders, where the power of your intentions and alignment with universal forces can unlock extraordinary success and fulfillment.

In the High AF Advantage method, we believe that harnessing your inner power and aligning with cosmic principles is the key to manifesting your desired outcomes.

By understanding fundamental cosmic laws, such as the Law of

Attraction, you can tap into the limitless potential of the universe and make your dreams a reality.

To place your cosmic order, begin by setting clear and focused intentions. Visualize your desired outcome and infuse your intention with positive energy and emotion.

Release any resistance or doubt, and trust that the universe is working in your favor.

By aligning your cosmic order with the four pillars of the High AF Advantage method—Igniting Peak Brain Performance, Flow State Sweet Spot, Cultivating Resilience, and Self & Success Mastery...

You can enhance your manifestation potential and create the life you've always dreamed of.

Ready to get your Transformative Groove on? <u>Connect with Nikki</u> now...Embark on a journey towards your New Reality!

JOIN THE MOVEMENT!

#BAUW

Becoming An Unstoppable Woman
With She Rises Studios

She Rises Studios was founded by Hanna Olivas and Adriana Luna Carlos, the mother-daughter duo, in mid-2020 as they saw a need to help empower women worldwide. They are the podcast hosts of the *She Rises Studios Podcast* and Amazon best-selling authors and motivational speakers who travel the world. Hanna and Adriana are the movement creators of #BAUW - Becoming An Unstoppable Woman: The movement has been created to universally impact women of all ages, at whatever stage of life, to overcome insecurities, and adversities, and develop an unstoppable mindset. She Rises Studios educates, celebrates, and empowers women globally.

Looking to Join Us in our Next Anthology or Publish YOUR Own?

She Rises Studios Publishing offers full-service publishing, marketing, book tour, and campaign services. For more information, contact info@sherisesstudios.com

We are always looking for women who want to share their stories and expertise and feature their businesses on our podcasts, in our books, and in our magazines.

SEE WHAT WE DO

OUR PODCAST

OUR BOOKS

OUR SERVICES

Be featured in the Becoming An Unstoppable Woman magazine, published in 13 countries and sold in all major retailers. Get the visibility you need to LEVEL UP in your business!

Have your own TV show streamed across major platforms like Roku TV, Amazon Fire Stick, Apple TV and more!

Learn to leverage your expertise. Build your online presence and grow your audience with FENIX TV.
https://fenixtv.sherisesstudios.com/

Visit www.SheRisesStudios.com to see how YOU can join the #BAUW movement and help your community to achieve the UNSTOPPABLE mindset.

Have you checked out the ***She Rises Studios Podcast?***

Find us on all MAJOR platforms: Spotify, IHeartRadio, Apple Podcasts, Google Podcasts, etc.

Looking to become a sponsor or build a partnership?

Email us at info@sherisesstudios.com

www.ingramcontent.com/pod-product-compliance
Lightning Source LLC
Chambersburg PA
CBHW051053050726
47592CB00002B/505